Let's Talk About Your Handicap

.

Let's Talk About Your Handicap

How to improve your Handicap in the sport of Polo

Sunny Hale

I dedicate this book to polo players who are seeking improvement in the sport of Polo and especially the ones who are in search of the answers that are hardest to find. This book is for you.

I also would like to say a special thank you to all the great players I had the opportunity to play for and against who taught me so much on the journey to living out my dreams in the sport of Polo. I will always be in gratitude for the experience and the adventure of a lifetime competing at the top of the sport with all of you, especially the ones with a great sense of humor!

CONTENTS

Finally…someone wrote it all down ☺!

~ 1 ~

A personal note from Sunny...

Polo is one of the only sports known to man that does not base its player ranking on some type of statistics. So where does that leave the individual who is in pursuit of reaching the top, with knowing how to get there? What does it really take to see your personal skills improve and that number representing your Handicap actually make a move on the scale?

I have spent the greater portion of my life so far in pursuit of conquering my dreams in the sport of Polo. As a result, I have logged a serious amount of hours and buckets of sweat in the discovery of what works and what does not, when it comes to improving as a player. Let me explain my dream in the sport of Polo and then you will understand clearly what I had to be able to put together in order to reach it. My dream in Polo was, "to play with the best polo players in the world, because they asked me to be there." That was it. That was my personal dream and I didn't want the spot given to me for any other reason, than I earned it. I always believed that if I did the work, I would get the invitation. What that meant on the work side of things, is that I needed to out rank every human on the planet at my Handicap, in order to get that opportunity and invitation. Ok…so that's what I went to work on until I achieved it. I wanted to leave no detail out when it came to knowledge and it was only because of my work ethic and pursuit of excellence, that I got what I was after in the opportunities to play at the top of the sport. I started out as a minus one with no financial fortune to back me and climbed my way through the ranks of the sport and tournaments, until I hit the beginning of conquering my dream. For over 20 seasons I was asked to play as a professional player for some of the greatest players of all time with the longest winning streaks and number of tournament titles won. I played for most of the top professional brother combinations and Champions in the sport including the Legendary Carlos Gracida who gave me my first 26 goal invitation, Memo Gracida, Eduardo Heguy, Benjamine & Santiago Araya, Pite & Sebastian Merlos, Owen Rinehart, Adam Snow, Julio Arellano and the world's number one player Adolfo Cambiaso to name a few. It took playing consistently above my Handicap, "being a ringer", to get the invitations I was looking for. Then when I got them, I had to step on the field and be able to perform. Game on…that was the fun part and I couldn't wait to get started each time ☺! So when I say that I know what you are going through in pursuit of improving, trust me, at one time or another I have faced it and why I felt it would be really helpful to share what I learned along the way.

Well, lets just say that's how it started in my mind, as

this simple little thought and idea. I thought, wouldn't it be nice to explain in simple terms everything I have learned about Handicaps and how to improve them? Then as I got farther and farther into writing this book I realized just how complicated the puzzle must be to put together for people who are just getting started or who have never had it truly explained to them by a professional who has done it themselves in their own career. Then I realized how many new players that I have taught over the years and have played with that don't have access to the right information or even a clear explanation of what a Handicap even means and what information it is based on. That's when I realized I had to do this book and provide some simple easy to follow answers. Make no mistake, Polo is a blast and the best school you will ever go to as you pick up all the clues to the puzzle over time, but it can also be very frustrating if you have a real agenda to improve and aren't seeing the results you would like to at the rate you would like to see them. It can also be very costly if you are spending lots of money on the wrong details that aren't producing solid results that you are happy with. That is one of the goals for me in this book, is to help you skip the un-necessary time spent logging hours in the wrong direction.

To be really good in the sport of Polo, you have to know exactly what you are after. Once you know that, then you can put in the time on mastering the correct things that will produce the results you are looking for. If you don't know what you are after in terms of the right things to work on, you will never hit the target you have in your mind. My point, do you know exactly what is involved in improving your Handicap? Do you know what will produce solid continued progress towards a potential Handicap increase? Do you know the basic ingredients in a Handicap? Do you know a successfully proven plan to improve a Handicap? These are things you have to know the answer to in order to be able to keep improving as a player and if you don't, you will be logging lots of hours on the wrong stuff that may or may not have any positive effect on you actually improving. Sure, you will still have a great time playing Polo, but will you truly improve as you would like to? No. By the end of this book you will be able to answer those questions and many more with confidence.

In order to have the best chance at a Handicap increase, you have to be able to do something really well to get noticed and exceptionally well to be able to have an effect on the outcome of a game. Being able to have an effect on the outcome of a game in a positive way is a big point in the wow department. The best players in the world have something extra, something special whether a God given talent or sheer hard work and sweat...they have something that makes them stand out.

When it comes to you improving as a player, the most important thing you can do first is to determine what exactly you would like to accomplish, so that you can have a target that you are aiming at. It might be a certain Handicap you are after, it may be to increase your current Handicap by a goal, or it may be to perfect one of the key ingredients that really interests you. Or, it may be to just truly understand the game better by learning the fundamentals to the ranking system. My point, choose something and let's get to work on it. If you can see the destination in Polo you want to get to, I can help you with the path to get there.

Becoming a great polo player has to do with how much effort you are willing to put into the task, so I hope you realize right up front this is not a book about one day, some day maybe…this is the book that will give you actual details and strategies you can start implementing today that can help you actually accomplish your goal. In order to improve at anything you have to have a desire to achieve something, no matter how small or large the actual detail, you have to have something that is bothering or poking you to go beyond what you already know. That is the truly engaging part of the sport of polo, because there is always something left undone or unknown that you will be left pondering after you play. Trust me, all players drive or head home after challenging games with something left burning on their minds. That nagging question…what if I had made this play instead of that play? What if I had used a pelham on my second chukker instead of a gag? What if I had backed the ball instead of turned it in the last play…so many questions…lol. That is my point. Everyone has them and that is what keeps you coming back for more. It is like the unsolved mystery novel that just keeps unfolding with more questions and suspense to solve the situation. That is what this book is all about. I am going to help you solve the mystery of what is holding you back from being a better polo player. Some of the things we will cover in this book you may already be aware of, but didn't have hard answers or tools to use to solve the issues and some of them you may never have realized.

Here is what I learned along the way in my professional Polo career in terms of a player's Handicap and how to improve. I warn you now, I have never seen where anyone has actually written it down with a simplified plan that is easy to follow, so we may be sailing into uncharted waters of top secret info on this chat, but I hope it helps you. I also hope this will be a useful guide that you can have to refer back to as time passes and your skill level changes, that can help answer your questions when progress levels off with no idea of why.

I only give you one potential failure warning about this book and its contents. It only works if you add "effort". Be prepared with this information right from the start. If you really do mean to improve, it will take some effort on your part to make a decision to go after it and then you'll need to get to work on the details one by one.

Due to the amount of detail that is buried in truly mastering the sport when it comes to knowledge and in order to not create a long novel that knocks a person straight to sleep, I have decided to give certain topics an entire book so I can really do them justice in explaining the inside details as I know them. So if you want more details and information on some of the things that I talk about in this book, then you will want to keep an eye out for the next books coming in the Let's Talk Polo book series when they are released at www.sunnyhalepolo.com.

This also means that some of the information has been summarized to help you get straight to the point and not get bogged down in too much un-necessary side info that can take away from a clear understanding.

Thanks for taking this adventure with me and get ready to see your polo start improving!

All the best,

Sunny

~ 2 ~

The Basics About Handicaps…

11

No matter how long you have played Polo, there is one topic that is almost never clearly explained to an extent that you can get a clear picture of what is involved. Well, that was before this book. That is the way it "used to be" before the introduction of this book. Starting right from ground zero on the subject of a player's Handicap we are going to start at the origin of a Handicap and then go all the way to how to improve it, with an end result of the reader closing the book with a solid understanding of all aspects of the Handicap.

What I am about to explain in this first chapter goes into some clear details and explanations that are often taken for granted among the polo community as common knowledge, which leaves the brand new player with a whole lot of unanswered questions. So, if you are new to Polo you will thoroughly enjoy this first chapter and finding out the answers to some solid mysteries you have been working with in your new endeavor to become a polo player.

Now let's get started ☺!

The Truth About Polo Handicaps...

Ok, let's start right from the beginning with the real facts. When it comes to a polo player's Handicap, an Official Handicap from a recognized polo association anywhere in the world, there are a few details you need to know going in. I will list them below so you will have a clear understanding of the basic foundation of information that gets the ball rolling on the subject. Keep in mind the sport of Polo is over 2,000 years old and one of the oldest organized team sports. That being said there are a lot of traditions that run deep in the sport and the player's Handicap is one of them

What is a Handicap? A Handicap is the term used in Polo to describe a player's ranking and skill level on a numeric scale.

Why the need for a Handicap? The Handicap is necessary for three primary reasons in the sport of Polo and the traditions of how things function within the sport.

1. The first reason is: in order to have the ability to separate and identify the skill level of players in head to head competition.

2. The second reason is: in tournament polo you need a way to identify the skill level of the team members as a combined group.

3. The third reason is: for tournament organization you need a way to be able to set specific tournament Handicap entry limits for team entry. This helps to keep the tournament competition as fair as possible and be able to eliminate any unfair mismatches between competing teams by the use of a Handicap difference on the board when you start the game.

The traditional numeric scale used: The most common numeric scale and range used for official player Handicaps within polo associations that you may register with is from (-2) to 10 goals, 10 goals being the highest attainable Handicap and best player possible. There are countries where the lower handicap numbers have a few more notches, but as of the writing of this book I have never heard of any country going higher than the 10 at the top of the scale. There are also countries that will assign a letter to any number on the scale that is "0" or less to overcome any negative connotation in discussing your rank. Sounds funny, but as far as I have ever known that is the real answer to the use of letters in place of negative numbers and have never seen anywhere or heard an explanation different than that one. So there it is, the rest of the story on the small details that never get explained.

The Handicap criteria guide to follow as you go: Now the bad news. There is no official guidebook that is made available to players with the breakdown or criteria for what each number on the numeric scale used to rank you with, actually refers to. Yes, that sounds crazy, but it is a fact. Remember, my aim in this book is to give you the facts, as I know them so as to demystify the whole Handicap topic. I would also like to say that I am not endorsing the idea of no official guide for a player to follow with the ranking criteria, I am just delivering the news so you will have all the information as I know it currently.

The statistics that equal a player's Handicap: More bad news. There are no guidelines for any designated statistics that equal a number or published player benchmark for you to find on the numeric scale either. Yeah, you might want to re-read that last sentence one more time. Sorry about that, I am just the messenger.

Who does the handicapping? Each country has an official polo association or governing body that runs and promotes the Polo within that respective country. Within a country's polo association there is an official handicap committee including a designated chairman, who is normally made up of volunteers that are also polo players, who are tasked with the actual diligence work to get to the actual numbers assigned. This is done through lots of discussion and reviews of player recommendations at annual meetings based off your performance in mostly tournament polo. The designated Handicap committee in each polo association that you will register with holds the magic wand and has the authority to grant you your number on the scale annually. Think of it like this. You know how beauty pageants are done? The models are ranked 0-10 and no one on the outside knows the scale, but everyone seems to know when a 10 walks across the stage? Yeah, it's like that. The problem that arises is all of the players who aren't the 10's have to be separated and assigned a number on the scale as fairly as possible, with a suitable Handicap that matches their ability against all of the other players in the association who have registered that year and that is the job of a handicap committee. Make no mistake this is a huge and thankless task to do each year and credit to those players who donate their time to voluntering to help solve the annual decisions. The committee decisions are made by its members and chairman after much deliberation for those players that have been seen fairly frequently. For the players who haven't been seen much by the handicap committee you are not going to create much chatter and therefore have a slimmer chance of making any move up the scale. Sounds crazy, but this is the tradition that still lives in Polo as of today 2016. This is a large job to accomplish for any committee and especially as there are no hard and published statistics to base the decisions on, it leaves the door open to lots of questions from players on why they are ranked as they are.

Can some Handicaps be political moves? Are there humans involved? Remember human nature exists wherever there is a human at work and Polo is no different. Not all Handicaps are political, but there are occasions where Polo-tics can sometimes play a role in a player's Handicap. However, the good news is that these Polo-tics can be overcome by having stellar and consistent performances on the field in tournament polo. I am an excellent example of the power of what can be overcome with the right work ethic and attitude about it no matter what your gender. My advice is that you should NEVER take the number assigned to you "personally". Just get to work on being your best and don't waste any un-necessary energy spent in the wrong direction on this topic. If you are handicapped wrong and too low, guess what then you are a legitimate "ringer" and will be highly sought after for teams. So either way it is really important to just keep doing the work to becoming your absolute best. The players who are willing to step up and volunteer, dedicate a lot of time to help on the committees and until you are ready to step up and start volunteering your time in the process or to help create a new process to update and improve the current, your are an armchair quarterback of a volunteer's efforts. Become the volunteer if you feel really passionate about this topic and help create the changes you'd like to see happen.

Does any description of a Handicap exist? I have traveled around the world playing Polo and hold Handicaps in several countries and have only seen a few times a small version of an attempt in certain places, to describe what a player should know how to do at a designated Handicap number. However, the papers I have seen only describe the Handicaps of a (-1) to a 3 goal player at the high numeric end of explanations, before the paper ends. That is the truth as I know it.

Handicap homework for future wizards: I say the word "wand" in good humor, as the Handicap committees in each association have quite a task to assign the correct Handicaps to players. Also, you may want to keep in mind this very under publicized fact that I will share with you that runs true in most countries around the world, that adds to what a big job each committee is tasked with. With the exception of Argentina, the majority of registered players to an association will end up being ranked at 3 goals and below. That is a whole lot of different style players ranked at only a couple numbers on the scale. That is why, especially without a written code to go by that is publicized to players and easy to find, it is quite a mystery to all who have signed up as they wait annually with anticipation to find out where they landed on the Handicap scale after a season of play. Without a clear explanation of why and how the decision was made, made public and accessible there is no way for a player to have a solid answer that is useful to them as an aspiring polo player. This is why it can be so frustrating for a player who would really like to move up the scale with some solid facts they can go to work on fixing or improving.

I believe it would be a great idea to have a few after game asado's around the globe to gather as many players as possible and create some discussion that leads to the creation of a future document with basic Handicap criteria guidelines for new players to be able to follow, but as of now you're out of luck except for what I am about to explain in this book and any other additional resource you may be able to dig up with some serious investigative work.

There may be a wizard somewhere in the world that has mastered the entire list of criteria -2 to 10 goals and benchmark skills that each player must have to hold a certain Handicap, but as of today and writing this book I have not met that wizard. If I should meet him or her somewhere along the way I will be sure to let you know, but until then let me help with what I do know about Handicaps and all that goes with them, that you may want to know when it comes to improving your number on the scale.

How Many Handicaps Are There?

If you thought there was only one type of Handicap, buckle your seatbelt, because I have some breaking news for you. There are a few different types of Handicaps in Polo, depending on what country you play in or what type of grounds you are playing on.

Officially recognized Handicaps: That being said, let's start with the Handicaps that are officially recognized and recorded by an official polo association. Generally speaking, there are three main types of Handicaps given by official polo associations and they are:

- ❖ The **Arena Handicap** (for use in arena polo only)

- ❖ The **Outdoor Handicap** (for use in outdoor polo only)

- ❖ The **Women's Polo Handicap** (for use in women's tournaments only and does not affect a woman's other Handicaps -Outdoor Handicap or Arena Handicap- at all.

Unofficial Handicaps: Now, unofficially there are some polo clubs that have created their own internal Handicaps to be used at their own clubs respectively for club play. These local Handicaps are usually created un-officially at small clubs in an attempt to address the compression issue of players within their local clubs. The compression issue amounts to a large number of players at one Handicap number that are not of equal rank. These internal club Handicaps are used to help the club run more evenly matched local tournaments and games to keep the games competitive and fair.

I have also heard of private associations that have created Handicaps for their own venues such as a beach polo handicap, due to the fact that the surface, size of the field and conditions can sometimes be very different from the official Handicaps criteria (as far as field dimensions) depending on the promotional company and what type of field they are able to create in the location.

Why the need for more than one Handicap? One issue is the size of the field you will play on that has a distinct impact on the style and speed of a polo game, therefore creating a different set of priority skills that a player must know and be able to execute to truly excel. For example, the most obvious and distinct difference in the arena and outdoor handicaps is the enormous size difference of the fields. How does this affect the player? In arena polo for example, the best players are the ones who are the bravest and quickest in making moves and risky plays in short spaces. The best arena player does not necessarily need to be a long distance ball hitter, but they must have exceptionally strong riding skills to be able to stop and turn with lightning fast speed in addition to quick and strong reflexes, as the distance they are dealing with is only about 300 feet in length give or take so things develop and change rapidly. As opposed to an outdoor player, who is dealing with a field that is 300 yards long. The outdoor player with exceptional finesse and ball striking abilities, that is able to read where the play will go before it happens and then be able to land a ball in that exact spot to a team mate at racehorse speeds will stand out above the rest. As you can see these are two entirely different focal points of specific skill sets for a player to master. There are many more unique examples, but that is one of the largest ones and easiest to spot watching a game. Make no mistake, a good polo player can play well on any surface or field size, but each of those two Handicaps were created to better assess the unique attributes of each venue in which the game is played, because it is a different style of play that is generated. It's two different styles of Polo and a separate Handicap for each unique style seems to work quite well around the world in keeping the player's balanced when they compete in each venue. With those two Handicaps, one does not affect the other and they are assessed individually each year annually by the handicap committee based on your performance in each type of Polo. One pattern regarding the two Handicaps that seems to be consistent around the world seems to be that your arena Handicap will be slightly higher than your outdoor handicap on average among players.

That being said, with the growth and popularity of new women's polo events being added around the world, there is now a third Official Polo Handicap being adapted in polo associations all over the world called, the Women's Polo Handicap. This relatively new Handicap is for use in women's polo events only and does not effect any other Handicap a woman may already have, nor is it used in anything, but officially recognized women's polo tournaments. It works in the same way as the other two and is for a specific type of event, women's polo tournaments only. As of the writing of this book there are 5 countries and growing, which have officially adapted this new Handicap to officially recognize the growing popular entity that women's polo has become and to be able to better address the extreme compression issue among this particular group of polo players in head to head competition.

How do you get a Handicap?

For those of you that are brand new to the sport, let's take it back a step and start from the very beginning. When you first begin to play polo, you will at some point be asked if you want to join a polo association for the country you are in. You might wonder is it necessary and what are the benefits if you do join? Some countries do not require you to join any association to play and some countries are very strict about encouraging people to join the polo association if they want to participate.

The largest reason a new player is usually inclined to join a polo association is at the point that they are ready to play in tournament polo and need an Official Player Handicap in order to enter the tournament. Most all countries require you to have an Official Handicap to enter an officially recognized tournament, so that the total team handicap can be calculated properly. There are many additional benefits to join an official polo association and you should check with the country you are in to learn about all of the benefits they have to offer. For the sake of staying on topic in this book we will focus on the single benefit called your official player's Handicap. Your Handicap gets initiated when you sign up to join the polo association as a playing member. That is where a Handicap originates and how you get one.

If you would like a little more detail on the actual steps that happen when you join an association and how it works, here is one example. In the USA, the process to getting a Handicap is fairly simple. Step one is to register with the polo association as a playing member. The next step will be a piece of paper you will receive for you to get filled out by a few designated people who have seen you play, who will recommend a starting Handicap. That paper than gets turned in to the polo association and goes directly to the handicap committee for evaluation. The handicap committee is who will make the final judgment and numeric decision for you. After you sign up for membership, you will receive your official membership card with your Handicap printed on it. After you have this designation, you will then be eligible to play in officially sanctioned or recognized association events. Your Handicap will be re-evaluated each year you renew your membership after that, to address the need for any fluctuations up or down the scale depending on your playing abilities as they progress or decline.

The good news about Handicaps

Now that you know the basic facts regarding Handicaps, I want to share some good news with you regarding the formula that I know works when it comes to improving them. The good news is this:

❖ The plan to improve an Outdoor Handicap, an Arena Handicap, a Women's Polo Handicap or a club created non-official Handicap… is the same one.

❖ The plan I am going to give you in this book will work for all of them and your success depends on how much you are willing to put into it.

❖ It's that simple ☺!

One more detail to know that will help you

Ok, here is the one additional piece of advice you need to know when it comes to the basics about Handicaps that will help you reach your highest potential and starts right from the beginning and should not be left out in your planning. In addition to the plan I am going to show you, the additional advice I would give that will help you reach your best potential Handicap increase or type of player you are going after, is this:

❖ Give specific practice and tournament time to the specific type of Polo you love to play and want to be best at. Your focal points overall are very important, so if you want to be the best arena player possible than spend time playing arena tournaments, especially improving and polishing your riding skills and your ability to create and solve strategic moves and line changes quickly and effectively as a main focus. Work on your short-range shots placement and your ability to play off a ball coming back at you from the wall at a rapid speed. Also work on your ability to shoot at goal from all over the arena and be accurate. You should be able to score from anywhere and know where the goal is blindfolded. You are working with short distances so there is no reason why you shouldn't be able to shoot goals from anywhere.

❖ If you are after reaching the highest Outdoor Handicap possible, than get to playing as much Outdoor tournament polo as possible where you will be forced to make moves and engage in new situations that challenge your skills and pull you out of your comfort zone at a rate you can keep up with safely. Work to master the position you think you are best suited for and eventually learn the roll of each position on a team, so that you can understand the entire dynamics a team needs to function with to succeed.

❖ Some additional tips about crossing over between arena and outdoor polo if you play both. Arena polo has a few distinct characteristics that will place players in a much more action packed situation that forces you to come out of your comfort zone with a lot of quick stopping and turning and player interactions due to the short distances you are traveling in a game. Arena polo will also force you to learn about quick and sharp line changes and force you to learn to be much more aggressive and physical if you want to get anything done or be a factor in the game. Over time those skills can add some real edge to your game. My point, if you are playing arena already or is all you have access to and aspire to be a great outdoor player...just wait, all the work you are putting in now in the arena will pay off big time when you go outdoors. You will be the player who is not afraid of the action when it shortens up and gets physical. Then you can just add your finesse and ball striking abilities to the foundation of what you have built in the arena. Arena to outdoor is a really fun transition.

My point. If you want to be great in the arena, play more arena polo. If you want to be great at outdoor polo, play more outdoor polo. If you want to achieve the highest Women's Polo Handicap, play more women's tournaments and tournament polo of any kind. The plan we are about to get into works for all three of the Handicaps I have explained, but the more specific you can become about what you want to accomplish, the better chance you will have to accomplish it. So get this clear in your own mind when you start and you will be able to find much more satisfaction as you go.

~ 3 ~

How to Improve Your Handicap

A solid foundation is the key to improving your Handicap in Polo and here is why. In order to feel true confidence you must know precisely how to perform a task or a skill and then be able to repeat it. Knowledge and proper execution of that knowledge is what builds a solid foundation of confidence. As a player, when you have that kind of confidence, your focus in a game becomes about strategy and how to get the most out of each play for your team or individually. When you have that kind of confidence you are also willing to take on new challenges against better players during a game and you are able to command respect and a space for yourself in and through plays. This kind of confidence is what you are seeking as a player who is on the move up the handicap scale.

Seeking answers to build your skill sets and knowledge is the key that unlocks the door to true improvement in the sport of Polo. To be a great polo player you have to know how to repeat all of the tasks and skills under extreme pressure in tournament polo. Eliminating doubt through knowledge and the ability to execute properly is what a solid foundation is all about and what we are going to go over in this book, so that you will have a clear understanding of what it takes to reach your best. What you do with the information and how far you go with it is then up to you.

Warning…when a player displays a certain skill they are good at or a play they can make really well and they get attention for it each time they are able to perform it, that player may be less likely to pay attention to mastering the whole equation and process in exchange for repeating that single wow moment they have as a player. Trust me, I know how it feels and I have to admit, it is fun to quick draw and shoot the bullet that you know will hit the bulls-eye on the target and hear the crowd go wild, but staying focused on repeating that single burst of greatness can also be the cause of a stunt in your growth more severely than anything else. Keep working on the equation as a whole and learning each of the steps in the plan and you will be loading yourself with tons of bullets you can start peppering everyone with on the field in the future, instead of just one. As a player, if you do something great that gets attention quickly you need to pat yourself on the back, log it and keep going at learning the rest. Remember I mentioned that fact and don't worry it's just us here chatting, it goes nowhere if that's already happened to you.

Improving your Handicap is a process of collecting lots of pieces of information. Think of it like playing one of those video games that you have to collect things for points or weapons as you go, in order to win. Yep…Polo is the same way. As you progress into a new level of tournament play you will find new information and a new level of pressure greater than the one you stepped up from. As you progress in horse purchases, you will find new information and learn lots of lessons and some will be expensive if you are not paying attention. Remember this next very important piece of advice. Information will come in two forms: good information that helps you immediately and information that comes in the form of a big mistake. As an aspiring polo player you need to collect both kinds of information to complete the puzzle of being the best player. The reason you need both is that you have to know what does not work for you, in order to know exactly what does. That is what the value of mistakes are all about, so if you have already logged a bunch of excellent mistakes, just realize all of them are helping to fine tune exactly what will work successfully for you as a player. These lessons will come in horses, in team mates, in positions you will play, in grooms you will hire, clubs you will play at, in equipment you will purchase, in people you will get advice from…all of it is a potential lesson to help you go forward. For example, with each new set of mallets you order, you will find new details like weight or flexibility variances you have to have that will give you advantages that you didn't know about before, when you ordered the previous set or special mallet. Each new groom you hire will bring new knowledge to you about yourself and your string. Some of it will be helpful and some of it may hold or set you back, but both kinds of information are needed in the process of improving as a player. If you are the groom, well guess what? Each time you play you need to be taking a mental note of the small details that seem to improve your results for the day, the results that get you to the simpler routines that produce a more efficient job for you and your horses and stop doing the stuff that makes your polo day more stressful.

How do you keep all the information simplified in your mind as you go? All of these things and many more are buried in the details of becoming a great polo player and you will go through all of them at one time or another on your journey, so get ready to absorb as much as you can. Here is a suggestion for you to keep the constant "all you can eat buffet of information there is in Polo" that you will need to know, limited to two plates of food for you to digest. For new experiences and information, separate them into two basic categories "useful, works for me and my horses" or "not useful for me, but now I know what to stay away from...thanks for that one I'll never do that again!" Then get going to the next step up the ladder of information. Sometimes you might repeat a lesson or two if you were unable to log the info correctly the first time, but try not to make it a habit of repeating the same mistakes and you'll be good to go.

Now, let's get started on the plan that I know works.

The 7 Step Plan That Works

Improving in Polo is about a constant quest for what you don't know or the skill you aren't able to perform. Once you can perform the skill or understand the knowledge you were missing, you have mastered the next step up the ladder to improving your Handicap in Polo. I know this plan I am about to give you works when it comes to moving up the Handicap scale and I hope it gives you a boost and platform to achieve your future goals in Polo. It takes time, but the good news is that there is a plan that can get you there with good results, so get ready here we go!

It only has one potential glitch…so be warned right up front. You have to be willing to put in the work. Yep, potential sweat and dirty jeans coming your way ☺! I know what kind of work it takes to truly improve, so I am not here to tell you a bunch of fluff that sounds pretty. I am here to give you the facts as I learned them along the way in my career. If you truly love Polo and want to improve, you will now be armed with the information to get you ahead in the sport as a player. I have thousands of hours invested in each of the details, so my goal in the book is to help you skip all the wasted time and efforts focused on the wrong stuff. Trust me, I made lots of mistakes and some really hilarious ones, so I am aiming to expedite your work in Polo by giving you the notes on what works, simplified into a 7 step plan, so you can reach your goal sooner than you imagined.

Just because you are spending time on the polo field does not mean you are adding value to your Handicap or skill level. That is what this book is all about. My goal by the end of the book is that you will be able to determine the places in your own program that you can adjust, add to or delete to help increase your personal progress. Take your time to understand each step clearly and you will be well on your way to solid improvement. That will hold true even if you just start focusing on one step at a time and just master it to the best of your ability. That single step will add so much confidence to the game you are already playing, that you will be amazed. Each task you master will unlock the door to new opportunities on the field and a new level of confidence in your game. That is when Polo gets turned up a notch in the addiction and fun that flows through your veins. Hopefully someone has already mentioned to you that Polo is addicting and there is no cure, but it's the best addiction you will ever have. Don't forget, I aim to give you the facts as I know them and that is a well-known fact.

Please keep in mind as you go, I actually used this methodology in my career to accomplish my goals so I am well aware of some of the thoughts you will be going through, because at one time or another I have had them all. With this plan and a solid work ethic to improve in every aspect of the sport, I went from playing dirt fields as a (-1) to a professional player at the top of the sport being sought after by the best players in the world in High Goal Polo for over 25 seasons. This plan is tested and for me was a complete adventure to figure out, as each major new lesson I had to learn sometimes came after some intense critique from top players and myself and some of the funniest situations. Like this one: You ever sat about 2 feet in front of a television with Eduardo Heguy holding the remote in dead silence and hitting replay until you realized he was trying to get you to confess and explain just what happened in the play with me and the 10 Goaler I was asked to mark for that particular play? Well I have. And yes, he is quite the prankster, but a great polo player. I learned a lot of great moves and strategy from some outstanding and historically famous players and I wouldn't trade it for anything. To me the experiences are priceless and like that one, some of them were down right hilarious and still make me laugh when I think of them.

This 7 step plan is the simplest way I can explain what needs to happen in order to improve your Handicap in Polo. They major benefit to the plan is that it provides a clear and easy to follow list of steps that are repeatable and through the right work ethic to practice them, will create a solid foundation. As you read, you may recognize that some of these steps you have already mastered in the overall process and that is great. Check those ones off and move to the ones that either look like brand new information or interest you to try and improve on. That is what's great about having it on paper, you can always go back and refer to the topic that still gives you trouble or creates challenges that have been stalling you out. The other benefit is that you will now be able to have a book of clues that will help determine what you are missing in your skills as an aspiring polo player.

Each of the 7 steps in the plan I will show you, plays an intimate and important role in the picture of a polo player as a whole, so remember that I said that. A top polo player is a player who has a well-rounded base of skills and can perform them under pressure, in tournament polo and in different environments and locations.

STEP ONE IN THE PLAN

Know the ingredients in a Handicap

For a lot of players who have been around polo their whole lives, it may come as common knowledge what the key ingredients are that make up a player's Handicap. But to the aspiring polo player who does not have that background, it is crucial to start right from the beginning so that you will know the scope of what needs to come together as a player in your abilities. In this chapter we are going to go through the ingredients one by one that I feel are the absolute foundation of a player's Handicap. There are tons of little details to add to them, but for the sake of not writing a long boring novel, this is the information that will form the basis of all that is to come in terms of your personal Handicap description. The number assigned to you now or in the future will be based on the performance or non-performance of the key ingredients that I will list for you in this first chapter.

Think of the key ingredients as your list of subjects to master along the way in your pursuit of excellence. Without a clear understanding of each of them, you will be severely challenged when it comes to a chance at a Handicap increase. Having this basic and foundation of information will set everything else in motion. Without this information you may spend years playing and getting caught up in the adrenaline rush of it all, without seeing much improvement. Don't worry if this has already happened, as it is a common issue among players all over the world. Polo is one of the greatest sports you will ever play and knowledge of what it takes to be good is just the beginning of all the fun to come. Here are what I consider to be the absolute key ingredients that make up a player's Handicap. Your potential as a player comes down to how many of these basic and foundational ingredients you can master. If you are missing one of these ingredients your car full of Handicap hope has a flat tire and needs attention.

1. Riding

2. Horses & Your String

3. Horsemanship

4. Your Hitting Skills

5. Your Knowledge of Strategy

6. Your Performance in Tournament Games

7. Your Mind

Once you have a clear understanding of the basic ingredients it takes to be good in polo, you can then get to work on the details of mastering each of them. The list above does not mean that there are no other factors involved, but what I want you to realize is that what I have listed above are the most important and largest factors to pay attention to if you want to be a solid polo player with room to grow. This basic knowledge alone can also help you out of a permanent plateau that you may have been stuck in. Think of them like this. If you are making coffee...they are your coffee and water. You can add all kinds of extras to make the coffee better, but without those basic ingredients you won't get far in your coffee shop.

To build a solid foundation, start seeking answers that will help build your confidence in all of your key ingredients. The habit of seeking answers and solutions to what is holding you back is how you build your foundation and confidence over time. A solid foundation means you have eliminated doubt and can move to the next step in new information and skills that used to look impossible.

It is also important to recognize that each of the basic ingredients has an effect on your overall picture as a polo player, so it will help you to think of your Handicap as a chain with six major links that are all connected. Then realize this fact. What is the value of one shiny link if it's not connected to the chain? That is the same with your seven main ingredients; they each have a purpose in the overall picture of a player's Handicap. You will do yourself a giant favor to understand how all six work together to complete the total package of a polo player.

Shine the individual links all you want, but at some point they all need to be linked together. That is what you are witnessing in a top player, with a high Handicap. A top player has all of the key ingredients functioning smoothly together. When one of the links is not so shiny it causes kinks in the performance and that can be seen very easily from the outside. I'll give you a clear example of what I mean. Have you ever watched a player who is amazing on the stick n ball field with hitting skills that would rival a 10 Goaler and you think wow, I can't wait to see this guy play he must be really good ☺! Then you watch him play and he is lucky to even get in a play and is hardly ever seen hitting the kind of shots you saw him take repeatedly on the stick n ball field all by himself. What happened? That is what I'm talking about when I say that all of your key ingredients have to work together and having one shiny link doesn't mean you will get crowned with a higher Handicap. And guess what, at some point they all have to work together in tournament polo under pressure. That is why the challenge of being a great player is so much fun to master and why there are only a handful of 10 Goalers in the world at any given time.

In the next chapter I will explain what each ingredient means, so you will have a better understanding of what is involved in the overall equation of a player and the important role each one plays in your Handicap, but for now take a mental note of that list and log it for later. That list is your homework to conquer as a player.

STEP TWO IN THE PLAN

Determine your weaknesses

Ok, now it's time to determine your personal construction zone and this time it is not just a specific skill we are after, but the whole enchilada. Everything that makes you the player you currently are versus the one you would like to become. The clues to what is holding you back lie in one or more of the key ingredients. Only you will know the exact answer, but I can help you by explaining all of the clues you are looking for in the hunt. That transformation is what this book is all about. And good news, you already hold most of the answers you will need to your improvement potential. That's what step two in the plan for success is all about, discovering your weaknesses so you can move up and into the player you want to be. I am going to show you how to start identifying the issues that are holding you back and show you why they are so important in the overall picture of you as a player.

Some of step 2 may not be pretty, but it is the step you have to take in order to truly see any change or improvement. This step is where you find out the news; you are either an armchair champion or a serious contender in the hunt for real improvement answers. Yeah, I did just say that. So get ready, because I feel it is one of the absolute most important steps you will take to improve at any Handicap.

Ok now the ugly news. At some point or another, you will need to realize it is IMPOSSIBLE to improve unless you find you have a weakness. A weakness is a potential rung on the ladder that states clearly, there is one more level up you are capable of climbing in your journey to success. If you can see or feel a weakness, it means you actually have more room to grow. If you think you are perfect, well then there is absolutely no room for improvement. So...if you are not willing to start exploring what might be a possible weakness in your own game, then you have no hope to get better. None, in fact reach around and pat yourself on the back for reaching your full potential, because you are already at it. Sorry, sometimes the truth stings, but it is the right answer if you truly want to hit your top potential. If you are reading this and immediately started to think of all the mistakes you sometimes make in your polo, I got news for that reader...you are going places! It is that reader that has major room for growth. When I say major room for growth, I also mean potential Handicap increase is definitely within your reach and here is why. If you can see room for growth, meaning skills you don't have yet, missed plays you wish you had the knowledge how to pull off, riding glitches you wish you could master, hitting issues that embarrass you on a packed stick n ball field, fixing that one horse that just isn't playing well, strategy talk with your team mates that you wished made sense, fouls you made that still haunt you to figure out...those are the kind of examples I mean when I say, you are the ones with LOTS OF HOPE for potential improvement and Handicap increase. The reason why is this. With each issue you are currently challenged by, there exists a potential solution. With each new learned solution, you now have mastered one more skill you will need to be a player who is just a step ahead of the one you are now. That is the way up the skills ladder in polo. The higher you climb up the skills ladder in polo, with a solid understanding and ability to execute what once confused you, the closer you are to a notch up on your Handicap. Now, aren't you glad you have a bunch of nagging issues, questions, insecurities and fears that were bothering you? Best news ever.

What I mean by determining your weakness, is to be able to be honest with yourself and just start looking for the real answers. They hold the answer to what you can do for homework to improve. There is no race to solve it all, so just take your time and address each one at the pace you are comfortable with until you start to feel some confidence in that area, then move on to another topic.

Here is how to find them. Start identifying the topics on the list of the key ingredients that are difficult for you to do or the things that jump out at you immediately in your mind as something you would like to improve on and that includes general knowledge about the topic as well. Now make a mental list or an actual written list of those things and let's call that your "construction zone". This will be a working list of what you feel you would like to be stronger at. Creating this list whether mentally taking a note or physically writing it down, will produce a solid chance for improvement and here is why. Once you have identified what is holding you back from your best game performance, then it's really clear what work needs to be done. It is this simplified and slowed down approach that will get you the farthest in Polo. You have to take a minute to slow down every now and again from the rush of it all and give it some true thought, so you will have a clear and defined vision of what you are working on. That is also the best way to save lots of lost time working on the wrong stuff that doesn't add much overall improvement other than logging hours participating. This is one of the most important and critical steps that you need to take if you truly mean to improve. This is not always the easiest one to face, but it is what will make you better. Sometimes you may need the opinion of a professional who has seen you play to help point out the weak parts in your game, so keep that in mind.

CONSTRUCTION ZONE

On second thought, let's make sure you hit this step with the most punch and results, so let me help you find your weak spots with you now. Yep it's just me and you here and you now have some homework to do. My goal in this book is to get your Polo headed in the right direction and I did warn you already that this is the section you find our if you are an armchair champion or actually mean to make some progress so here we go, you're about to find out your answer. While we are on the topic and its fresh in your mind, go through each of the key ingredients listed on the next page and make a small note in writing what you would like to improve on for each of the them. Maybe you recognize there is something in each ingredient you want to improve on or maybe there is just one topic you really want to master. Either way, start to look at it like this and things will start improving faster than you know, because it will become a mental note on your mind instead of getting buried and lost in the shuffle of it all. That is how you attack progress at full throttle!

It's really important to mentally recognize the things in each category that stand out right away that you wish you knew more about or were more confident in…that is where you start. If you feel solid on all of them then good news, you can close the book you're 10 Goals.

CONSTRUCTION ZONE NOTES

Date: _____

1. Riding

   _____

2. Horses & Your String

   _____

   _____

3. Horsemanship

   _____

4. Your Hitting Skills

   _____

5. Your Knowledge of Strategy

   _____

6. Your Performance in Tournament Games

   _____

7. Your Mind (on the field in a game)

   _____

This will be your list to look back at later on and check your progress. It will also shock you if you do fill it out how much you truly have to work on and why you are not improving at the rate you would like to. When you put it together like this it is easy to see how many things you want to improve on and gives you a personal roadmap what you are after. Polo is very addicting and it is so much fun when you are out there playing and riding or stick n balling with friends that sometimes you just get caught up in the rush of it all and lose sight of the path you were on in improving and that is another reason why your progress gets slowed down once you have been in it a while. That is why it helps to take a few moments every so often to re check your progress and your input of work on the focal points you listed. As time goes when you look back on this list you will also be amazed to see the progress you have made…that is if you actually fill it out and are brave enough to put a date on it. This will be like your personal Polo journal of notes. If you want some constant reminders for yourself and are one of those players who wants the fastest rate of progress, then throw this book in your Polo gear bag and take a peek at this list when you're putting your gear on at practice to keep yourself really dialed in on the prize.

This little exercise can also be quite an eye opener, as these are the frustrations that you carry around in your head as a player and it's quite funny to see how many there actually are when you list them out. That is why becoming a 10 Goal player is such a unique and honored place to reach in a player's career and why there are so few of them in any given year. To reach the top of the sport in Handicap takes serious dedication and focus on improving every time you go to the field or the barn and that is why the best players hold that spot.

If you take some time to think of your progress like this, even if its only one small item at a time, you will begin to discover a clear pathway forward in your improvement and you will literally have your own personal GPS how to reach what you are after. This is also the best way to keep a gradual improvement going and actually becomes quite a confidence builder as you go about mastering each one on its own. Do not feel you need to attack them all at once in a big hurry, just make a clear and defined effort at addressing whichever topic you decide to start with and then keep it going with one small detail at a time. Always set a pace that works for you to be able to keep up with, depending on the frequency of your access to Polo, horses, riding, games and budget.

With each improvement, no matter how small it may seem in the whole equation, you will add a new piece of confidence. That confidence is a rung on the ladder that leads to the top. In order to improve your Handicap, you have to take all of those small steps in order to get a solid understanding of each one. That is why it is important to identify your weaknesses. Those weaknesses left unaddressed will be a pool of doubt on the field, when the game heats up. Which means, you will skip those plays or be less likely to engage and that is not how you improve. Improving is about finding new knowledge and learning new skills, not just bypassing the scene all together. Skipping plays also adds to a player getting stuck at a certain Handicap. That's why you want to single out your weaknesses and then go to work on improving them one by one. This will be one of the largest beneficial moves you can make for yourself. It can also be one of the most rewarding when you use the plan I am describing, because it creates a solid foundation for self-improvement that you can continue to use throughout your polo career. This plan is not just for one Handicap of player, it is more like a general plan that can help a player at any Handicap redefine what needs work in their personal situation so they can continually have a target they are aiming at.

STEP THREE IN THE PLAN

Do your homework

How well you can perform each key ingredient plays a major role in your overall performance on the polo field and your Handicap potential. Once you have determined what your weaknesses are, the next step is to go to work on your construction zone and start knocking out the doubt and unknowns, one small detail at a time.

My entire goal in Polo was achieved through this process. One skill at a time, one shot at a time, one game strategy at a time, one horse training or fitness piece of knowledge at a time…they all head to be learned. The fun part to me was the challenge each detail represented to try and be able to do really well. I truly believed if I did the work my dream was possible. In fact, attempting to master this one amazing move I had seen a high goal player doing my first season in Palm Beach, landed me my first try out and eventual job playing as a professional player in the 22 goal for one of the biggest teams and organizations of the time at the original Palm Beach Polo & Country Club. I learn by being inspired. I see something that lights me up and I'm all over it. Well, I had seen this high goal player run a ball on the nearside in a half moon circle the width of the field at FULLSPEED across the middle of the field and when he hit the opposite side of the field, he necked the ball up field to his team mate with this deadly accurate pass. It was the coolest thing I had ever seen. I thought, wow…that was a move I needed to be able to make! So the very next day or it may even have been that same evening I can't remember, but I do remember I was all over it. I took my horses to the stick n ball field in the evening when everyone had cleared off and I went to work on trying to reproduce what I saw that guy do. I was a disaster on hoofs for the first 2 or 3 horses worth of stick n ball, as I attempted this running left turn on the nearside and neck-shot finish. I must have looked like a complete nut, but I didn't care, I really wanted to see if I could do it, because wow would that be cool to be able to do in a game like he did. So I kept going at it and drilling a hole in the field with these large running left turns for about 3 or four horses worth of stick n ball and some epic failures. So funny how many times and ways you can mess up one single play. Well I made them all, into the fence, into my horse, completely missing you name it I hit everywhere it's not supposed to go until…one round of the circle I MADE IT. Oh my God I thought…I can make the circle…if I can do it once, I can do it twice. Well then I did it! I completed the running circle carrying the ball on my nearside and the last part to master was that amazing neck-shot to finish the play. As I had been changing horses I noticed two guys sipping mate in the center of a barn aisle that was adjacent to the stick n ball field.

Everyone had gone for the day except them, as it was late afternoon early evening. That's the time of day I liked to go stick n ball and why I waited so long that day to try out the new move, so no one would be out there and I could have the whole field to myself to try this monstrously cool new play. Well, these two guys who I had never met just kept sipping mate up there in the barn aisle as I went about my business ripping up the stick n ball field and my poor horses were half dizzy from turning left. But then…IT HAPPENED!!! I managed to pull it off …the entire move. A running circle to the left carrying the ball on my nearside and a dramatic hard hit neck shot to a designated spot down field to finish!!! Wooooohoooo…I was the happiest camper ever!!! So of course, I had to make sure I could repeat it and kept going on Shameless, my gelding who was so nice to hit on and then it happened again…and again…and all of a sudden, the two guys who used to be sitting in the barn aisle were now at the fence line of the stick n ball field with a hand in the air waving me to come over to them. When I approached them I will never forget the look on their faces, it was one of the oddest and funny looks I've ever seen and I didn't understand it at the time, but they seemed nice enough so we sat and chatted a few minutes. That conversation turned into an invitation to try out for a 22 goal all Argentine team. Well, I got the job and the rest is history.

My point...go to work at what inspires you in the sport, or the items that you are missing on the list of key ingredients, or the specific details you have listed in your personal construction zone. Really work at giving time to each item that you aspire to be better at and you will start to see major improvement in your game. If you continue this kind of focused work ethic, no matter how slow the pace, there is no telling how far you can go. Each new skill you add to your key ingredients will add a new item to your toolbox as a player that you will have to draw from in a game. That is your homework. Keep at it until you are satisfied. Those new skills and bits of knowledge, no matter how small they may seem today or in the big picture of a polo player, are the answer to how you climb up the handicap scale over time. Each skill you master and each new piece of knowledge you gain in all of the key ingredients, is one step above the player you currently are now. That is how you consistently improve yourself as a player.

Now for the rest of the story on the two fellows who waved me over to the fence line while I was making my horses dizzy trying to pull off that cool play on the nearside. Years later at a barbeque we were talking about that experience when they first met me and the story came out. Turns out, the reason the two guys had come down to the fence line that day was because they were watching me stick n ball and one said to the other as they sipped their mate'..."Hey look, its Rob Walton stick n balling." The other one said, "that's not Rob Walton…that's a girl." That is why they walked down to the fence and waved me over, to see who was right. I had been wearing a ball cap and ponytail flying and one of America's top players at the time was Rob Walton who was a fantastic 8 Goal player with long hair. Now, years later I finally understood the looks on their faces. It is so funny thinking back over how some of my opportunities arrived. So if you are a young player with big dreams of becoming a professional in the sport reading this book, just get to work. Your goals are possible if you are willing to do your homework in every area.

Your future Handicap potential relies on this one fact. You are worth as much as the work you put in. If you are not willing to do the homework, you are done right where you are. You have reached your full potential and will be the same player tomorrow as you are today.

Do your homework; your handicap potential is determined by how much you are willing to put into it. It's that simple.

Now get busy on your construction zone and make sure to have some fun while you're at it ☺!

STEP FOUR IN THE PLAN

Test yourself

You're going to like this part. This is the license to grow your addiction, kind of like a prescription, you might want to cut this section out in case you need an excused absence note, for anyone who needs to see it. This is a big part of the plan to success as a polo player and must be done to know how you are doing on your homework.

Yep, test your homework and see if you are making progress. This is the most fun part of the plan. To test yourself means you need to sign up for tournament polo. Tournament polo is where the heat gets turned up and you get challenged. Being challenged is where you are forced to grow and expand your comfort zone. Each time you expand your comfort zone, you will have gained a new layer of confidence in your skills. This is the only way for a polo player to truly see a number increase in their Handicap.

Play all the practice games you want, but they don't force you to do anything except what feels good that day. You can engage or disengage whenever you want and with no pressure from team mates or umpires watching your every move. My point, there is no fire alarm going off, so no need to move your ass unless you feel like it.

The more you can test yourself, the sooner you will start seeing improvement, because with each tournament game your attention to detail or a certain detail will increase. Attention to that detail in your homework after the games will produce a solid new skill that you have mastered. Tournament games are what push this expansion and learning process forward full throttle. That is where you find out just how well your practice and work ethics and efforts are paying off. You have to be challenged in order to grow. There is no other way.

Practice all you want, but you have no real chance of improving your Handicap if you don't get out there and challenge what you know matched against other players. Your skill level has to be fine-tuned and sharpened and it is tournament games where it happens. Each tournament game that you come off the field thinking wow I just got my ass kicked, is a great chance to find out what you are missing so that it doesn't happen again. That is where the real lessons come from. Not from speculation, but from real situations that you get the opportunity to take part in physically. If you have the skill you pull it off and if you don't, you get your ass kicked. That's how it works and it's pretty simple to figure out what you're still missing. I'll give you a hint...it's that detail you can't get off your mind as you drive home after the game. That's your next homework assignment. Now get to work on it.

You see, there is no real loss suffered in a practice game and therefore no urgency to make many preparations or get any particular task completed proficiently. People can be polite and let plays go and you think you're doing great, because there doesn't seem to be much pressure against you. Don't fall for it; it's a false alarm in the confidence department. Yes, it is a good thing to feel great in a practice game, but until you are playing for an actual result that you are invested in you will not be challenged mentally and physically in split second decisions and skills executions. That is the test you need to take and as often as possible if you are in the real hunt for a Handicap increase.

Tournament time is also a total blast, when you go to the field and with your team mates you strategize and try to figure out how to overcome someone else's plan on the field with all of the skills you have and what you have in the arsenal of your strings. This is when Polo gets turned up a notch and completely drowns out the world and what is going on in it, due to the amount of detail involved in doing it well. In order for a team to do really well, everyone must be firing on all cylinders and paying attention. That is when your skills will be tested to the max and need to be extremely fine tuned and ready to go on attack. You will also be testing your mind skills to be able to work with your teammates efficiently or not at all. This is part of the test as well.

Tournament games are also where you find out how you are doing in the horse and riding department. Tournament games force you out of your comfort zone on the back of a horse, because of the pressure to get things done in the window of a chukker that is being timed. Tournament games are also where you find out if the fitness program you have for your horses is any good or needs work so that your horses can perform better. Tournament games also bring out the mistakes you are making in bridle combinations and schooling efforts. It is really easy to wing it in a practice game, but until you have to grab leather for the breaks, like happens in a tournament game, you haven't really tested anything in your horse program.

Tournament games are also where you learn about true confidence in yourself or the large ocean of doubt that exists when the heat gets turned up. These are things you have to know and start to be aware of in order to improve. To get rid of the ocean of doubt within you, you have to add new pieces of knowledge that solve the unknowns. Doubt equals an unknown. You either lack experience in the play or the ability to execute the play. That is where doubt lives and to dry up your ocean of doubt you must fill the ocean with new information and the ability to execute things with confidence, one small item at a time. That is what tournament games do for you, they shine a bright light on what still bothers you or gets you intimidated. Without this kind of trial there is no way to find your full potential as a player. Here is an example of what I mean in the amount of pressure and how it motivates you in different ways to perform. When you sign up for weekly club practice how does it make you feel...like the moment after you make the call to the polo office or send the email? Now, when you say yes to play a tournament game and send in your entry...now how do you feel? Like the minute you commit to the team...yeah...that feeling? Do you see what I mean? There is distinct difference in the immediate sense of pressure and adrenaline rush when you commit to a tournament and that adrenaline rush is where and how you get tested.

Tournament games are also the place to test your knowledge and execution of strategy. Strategy is for me one of the absolute most fun topics and skills to master and here is why. If you can be really good at strategy you can often win games and plays by knowing what the expected patterns of behavior are and being able to bring people into places they don't know answers for which turn into ball turn overs in your favor. Did I already mention I love strategy? Well I do. You can also save hundreds of wasted yards running on a field for your horse if you know the destination of the play that is developing and the timing that the ball will be in the intended destination. Translated it means you know the shortcut to where the play will be without having to follow the pack. This is a learned skill and one that all top players possess. Strategy is the key to stuff that looks like magic to the untrained eye observing a game. Tournament games are where you find out how many levels of strategy you are aware of and can execute. Yes, there are several levels of strategy and you have to learn each one in order for them to make sense. Just like going through the classes in school you start in the first grade and advance to high school and each grade is supposed to give you one more step of the foundation in basic knowledge. The knowledge you will pick up in Polo is similar and especially when it comes to strategy. K, I just decided strategy needs its own book, as there is so much fun stuff to explain. For instance, when you first start playing polo someone might tell you to go mark a player and make sure to do it on their "right side" or "hitting side". The strategy at that level is to just take away the option for a newer payer to be able to hit the ball, due to the fact that most new players only have one side they are able to hit on and that is the "right side". By doing this move you have taken away the other player's offense completely. When you progress in the sport to a higher strategy level, you will be asked to do the same task, but this time you will be expected to know which is the correct side to make contact with them on based on where you are on the field. The idea in a more advanced strategy option is to "own the center of the field" by pushing your opponent to the outside or boards when you make contact. These are two distinctly different strategies to the same task and the reason why sometimes it's easy to get confused on proper play execution if no one is barking orders or breathing down your neck to explain, as they will do in a tournament game. Tournament games bring out all the questions including ones like the example I just gave and that's why you need to play them, so you can to get to the answers.

Tournament games challenge every key ingredient and every ounce of homework time you have put in and they are what will give you your final grade on how you are doing, so my advice is to start planning when your next tournament game will be, even if you have to go at the pace of one tournament per year. Pick one and start planning. That energy is what will inspire you to go to work at improving to get ready for it and that is how you become the best polo player possible.

Tournament games will test hundreds more details than I have mentioned here in this chapter, but these examples I have pointed out should give you a pretty clear example of why the step to sign up for tournament polo and test yourself is such a huge part of the plan to your success as a player.

And ps...if you're getting in trouble for the amount of tournament polo you are playing...you can blame it on me. Tell them Sunny said you have to do it and it's her fault, and then get to your next game ☺!

STEP FIVE IN THE PLAN

Expand your growth potential

Here are three great ways to expand your growth potential as a player when you go to the field in practice or tournament polo. When I say expand your growth potential what I mean specifically, is that with each new level of pressure you put on yourself, you are forced to look for new solutions that you didn't have before in both physical answers and in wisdom of the correct answer. Look at it like a new door you are opening to a whole new library of information you will begin to learn about. This kind of specific targeting will help you become a stronger player and over time will help to increase your Handicap potential as you conquer each new challenge. Conquering each new challenge in this department is what will make you a more skilled player who can perform well under pressure.

Each of these three exercises will flood you with new information and questions that you did not have before. This new gap of "unknown's" is the room you will have to expand into as you learn the answers to the new knowledge and skills. This type of focus is great for the overall performance of a player who is seeking improvement on a consistent basis, as these can be used throughout your polo career to turn the heart up on your speed of improvement.

START MARKING BETTER PLAYERS
AT PRACTICE

When you go to your next practice game, start matching yourself up against better players than yourself and watch the transformation start to happen. That means when the game starts you should have someone in mind picked out that you will be attempting to mark for the entire game in all the set plays as your start point. Attempt to keep up with them, move for move and if it's a really casual practice, then just attempt to shadow them in every one of their moves off of the end line in set plays and down the field on defense, just as if it was a tournament game and that was your man. With each new level of effort you force yourself to step up into, you will find a new level of adrenaline, fear and doubt all crowding your thoughts as you attempt to match the player stride for stride in the plays you choose to give it a try. Maybe you'll get him or her and maybe they'll slip away from you, but what will for sure start to happen is that you will have moved off of the plateau you were parked at. It's like stepping out into the deep end of the pool the first time. It will freak you out at first, but as soon as you figure out how to float you will now not be so thrilled and excited in the shallow end anymore. The shallow end won't give you the same kind of high the deep end now gives you. That is how to view this kind of expansion. It takes time, but with each notch of player you get brave enough to try to match yourself up against and actually pull off a move or two on them,

75

you will be surpassing your old self and expanding your play capabilities. That is how you start to expand your potential in the performance on the field department.

This is best done in practice games, where there is not too much at stake if you completely fail the first time, because it freaks you out to be inside that player's strike zone or you actually run right over their line as you tried to match their slick moves on the horse. You don't have to go after the 10 Goaler first, just start picking someone on the field in the practice to match yourself up with that is a little more than you usually go after. Start there. Or, maybe choose to start with just one particular play you are going to make on or with the better player and make yourself keep up with them stride for stride. For example, pick a better player than you normally mark and attempt to just stick with them as the play starts on each of their knock-ins. Focus on that one task just as if it was a tournament. Do your best and see what happens. You will be surprised at how much effort and rush will go into that one play. That rush and focus is what will expand you personally in your skills execution and confidence levels over time and it can be done one play at a time or one level of player at a time.

My point is, this. If you always attempt to mark the same players in practice, or maybe you haven't actually realized how important it is to be doing that as a consistent habit yet, you will plateau often and will have a tremendously slow rate of growth if any. You will be like watching paint dry in the wow department. Handicap increases are about what you possess in the wow department, no matter what your Handicap is. You have to create chatter about your game in the actions on the field. Good chatter that is. This kind of personal practice habit will get you headed in the right direction. Once you see what I mean you will be hooked on picking new players to mark each game or practice to improve your confidence and the ability to execute precisely, when you know the target for the day.

Now, imagine what that one skill and bit of confidence could add to your next tournament game performance.

ATTEMPT TO PLAY A DIFFERENT POSITION
ON THE TEAM

This can be quite a fun challenge if you have never played more than one position before. Most players who have been in the sport for a while have been asked or forced to play different positions on the team and as a result have a pretty good understanding of the role of each player in a game. They also have become aware, due to the experience it provides, of the positions they enjoy to play and which ones they are not so much suited for. This is a tremendous benefit to learn about yourself and at some point needs to be solidified if you want to reach your highest Handicap potential.

If you are really comfortable playing a particular position that's great, you may have already found the position that best suits your style of play and horses. But if you have not been able to try playing any of the other positions and do not yet have a clear understanding of each role that position is responsible for, you may want to attempt playing an unknown position in some of your next practice games to start opening the door to new information about how strategy comes together in each position, by proper execution or complete failure to do so. This new experience will also help point out what you can do better in the old position you were playing, by what you need your new team mate (who is playing your old position) to be able to do to help you in your new role. My point? Get some strong coffee and re-read that last sentence until it makes sense and then take a few practice games and mix it up for yourself in what position you play for the day. Really attempt to master the position and if you're not sure of what to do just ask someone who is better than you who is out there for pointers. Most players are super open to helping other players with what they know, once you make the initiative to open your mouth and ask them. Lots of hours are wasted in practice games where no one ever opens there mouth to speak to each other and just lets the game role out in this unsaid sea of silence, except for the major hiccups and chatter among friends. This is a big step to take, but a really useful one in the player who wants to find their best-suited position, where their true skills can shine the brightest. It can also be a little humbling, so just remember I pointed that potential out to you too, when you decide to give it a try. But make no mistake, humbling is where you are forced to take a step in the direction of education or a final decision on the position that will be right for you. Either way, using practice games for this kind of an exercise will take your Handicap potential to a whole new level.

MOVE UP A HANDICAP LEVEL IN
TOURNAMENT GAMES

Each time you challenge yourself to learn something new you will be forced out of your comfort zone and normal habits into making new choices. These new choices will lead to things you have no idea how to do or let's just say, not so well just yet. That is how you open the door to improvement and without it there is no need to change from the player you are today.

When you first start playing polo, each and every game experience is like the rush of a lifetime and your adrenaline will be at full throttle. Your eyes are wide open and your heart is racing to figure out where you are supposed to be as a team mate and hoping all along to score a huge goal along the way or at least nail a big hit down field. Yeah...everyone gets this kind of fun racing through them at some point. That is the feeling you experience with each new and higher level of polo that you take a step up to in tournament games. For example, when you go from playing 2 goal polo to 6 goal polo you feel like you just went from 0 – 60 miles an hour in difference to the adrenaline level you are now receiving. That is the same for someone going from 12 goal polo to 16 goal polo. Each major jump in Handicap level of a tournament represents a whole new level of team strategy that needs to happen to keep up with that skill level of players and horses. What that means to the individual player is that your job just got more precise. Yeah, that means your riding skills are now going to be challenged harder, because you are up against a little tougher opponent who may be a little more slippery than the level you just came up from. Your hitting needs to be a little sharper to actually get your passes to your teammates when they call for them. The whole game will seem like it's way faster, which means you have a flood of extra adrenaline where you had been quite comfortable before. This is where your game begins to expand. After the initial freak out of adrenaline and fun and the dust settles, you will now be ready to look at a whole new menu of things you want to be able to do or at least try. This is how you expand your abilities by being challenged in a new level of play. With each tournament game and especially each jump up in the level of tournament game you are playing, you will be adding one more notch on your belt in strategy, speed and overall game performance abilities. This type of step up is what adds to your growth in terms of the complete package of a player on the move.

When you decide to make the jump, my advice is to start small. If you are a brand new player, maybe your first goal is to enter a tournament. If you have been playing a while in 0 goal polo, start looking for a 1-2 goal tournament to enter. If you have been playing 4 goal polo pretty consistently and feel pretty solid, start looking for a 6 goal tournament. If you have been playing 8 goal polo and below for a while start looking for a 10 to 12 goal tournament to enter. When a player makes a jump from 16 - 20 goal it is a huge step as the amount of players on the field who are supercharged in horses and skills increases, which means you need to get ready to step up your game in a big way to keep up. It is the same kind of leap when you go from 22-26 goal polo, a huge difference in finesse, strategy execution among team members and the greatest separation in power of horse player combinations can be felt.

This exercise and lesson will hit you in a secondary way when you step back down to the level you were playing before you took the leap up…and it will feel like you have way more time to make plays than you used to. That is part of the benefit as well. You will now have gained some realization of new confidence in your old settings. This is also a huge benefit to a player's overall performances and knowing what they possess in confidence under pressure. You need to know your strong points as a player to build true confidence and this is one of the greatest ways to expand yourself as a player at all levels of the sport. Remember, I started as a -1 on dirt fields and arenas and have played all the way up to 30 goal practices invited to play with the best players in the world in Argentina who were preparing for the Tortugas Open Finals and up to 26 goal tournament polo as a professional, so I know what its like with each step up in handicap level of a game. It's a total rush and so much fun to figure out. So get to scoping out your next tournament and give it a try.

STEP SIX IN THE PLAN

Learn to critique your performance

In a positive way that is ☺! This is one of the hardest skills to master. The hardest part is not to take your mistakes personally and let them crush your try.

"The hardest separation to make in your mind, that will open the road to solid improvement, is between self judgment which is basically our ego, versus being excited to discover hidden clues to improvement potential. "

You might need to reread that quote then stop for a second and think about it, because this is a huge concept to get right. Trust me on that fact, it is a fact and it will add a lot to your growth potential. When you start evaluating things you discover using the thought pattern that each new mistake you discover is a clue to improving yourself as a player (and especially as you are actually in the act of playing a game), you will have just mastered the hardest step to improving in the sport. That step is to train your mind to always be open and looking for improvement as opposed to letting your mistakes ruin your attitude because of your ego getting offended when you mess up. Take a minute to digest that concept, it's a good one and it works.

"Open for improvement means you put your ego aside and keep looking for clues to how you can get even better, especially in the heat of a game."

In fact, in the heat of a game is the absolute most critical moment to be able to critique yourself without taking it personally, because the minute you do take it personally you will for sure miss the next play or two as a direct result of frustration and grumbling about what just happened. If you want to be the best, you can't afford to waste time and energy on the field in a tournament game with useless behavior patterns. Remember you only have about an hour or hour and a half to play the game depending on the level of tournament you are playing. The more minutes you spend with the wrong perspective about critiquing your own performance, the more minutes will go in the trash in your overall game performance effort. All true champions in any sport know that fact. Polo is one of the absolute most challenging and fun sports, because of all of the moving parts in the basic elements that must work together to be really good as a player. That is the challenge that is so much fun.

Your mind learning how to view the mistakes in your game with the right attitude is the key to real growth no matter what you already know or how little you know. Believe me, I had some hilarious awesome stupid things I used to do on the polo field, before being tested over and over made them so obvious that there was no way to ignore them if I truly wanted to take the next step up in ability and skill level.

Every time you make a big mistake that is really noticeable it has an effect on your game. You might get upset, get embarrassed, get scared, get pissed off and lose your marbles for a few chukkers or just get frustrated and stay away from the topic or actual play all together for a while. Learning to self-critique your game, as it is in progress and after the fact with the proper and helpful attitude will open all kinds of doors to improvement that you may have never thought were possible before. It will also open you up to more energy spent in the right direction as well.

Don't make me laugh by thinking you never self-criticize yourself when you play. Seriously…everyone does it, so let me help you point it out a little more clearly for the shy or egomaniacs that may be reading this lol. You know that little guy that lives on your shoulder and screams in your ear when you make a huge foul. Yea, we're talking about that little internal dude's attitude. That is exactly what I am pointing at when we are talking about critiquing yourself properly during the game.

"That internal guy needs to change his story the next time to be screaming…next play get a move on it…we can talk about it after the game!"

87

Until you learn the value of using that mindset, summed up in the simplest quote I could think of to explain it clearly as your model of critique, you will run into roadblocks that don't seem to be fixable.

It is a fact. The correct critique by yourself can mean all the difference in the world to your game potential over time. Remember you're just looking for clues to your mistakes, once you know what they are, get a move on it and don't let them happen again. That is what constructive great self-critique is all about. If you have pros to help you out that is a great tool as well, but if you don't then you will need to go to work on this step as it is so powerful and holds so much hidden potential.

Ok, since it is just you and me chatting here I will confess an absolutely fantastic example of stupid excellence that when discovered helped me have one of my best games ever and it is because of the perspective I took when I discovered my mistake. Instead of letting it ruin my game and attitude, I used it as rocket fuel to fix the issue immediately and I mean yesterday fast. Here goes…true story. Let me share a personal example of an experience that required severe honesty in personal critique and absolute embarrassment in what I had to explain to the absolute best player in the world about my mistake during a game. The game happened to be a 22 goal Finals. Yea, great time to make a giant mistake on the number one field Sunday game in Palm Beach Florida and a few thousand spectators. My mistake had to do with focus and attention. I had thought it went unnoticed until the after party at the barn with a private asado celebrating a huge 22 goal undefeated league and finals victory. Here goes. In the finals match, I had been assigned by my team captain and best player in the world, two separate tasks to do. One on defense and one on offense and they went like this. When our team was on defense in a knock-in, my job was to mark Memo Gracida who was bringing in the ball for the opposing team. My job and focus was to force him to hit away, so that he didn't bring the ball all the way down field and my team captain could have a chance to steal his pass, that was job #one. My second job was for when we were on offense and my team captain was bringing in the knock-in, to go mark Memo's team mate Carlos Gracida. Set a pick on him so my team captain had a second to go by him with the ball without interference from Carlos. That was job#2. Simplified, on offense I had one task and on defense I had one task. That's pretty straight forward and I was ready for the job and couldn't wait to get started the day of the finals. Well, I was doing great the first chukker...I thought. Except I noticed an issue in my team, the team captain and second in command (a 9 Goaler) were arguing like crazy in Spanish and it was heated right from the get go in the first chukker. The second in command 9 Goaler had quite a reputation for yelling at young pros himself, but this time he was on the receiving end getting chewed on like a piece of corn at a summer fest in the Midwest and it was only escalating as the chukkers continued. In fact, it got so heated that a few mallets got sent through the tent and then it was evident something was really wrong with the two of them. I stayed out of it and kept focusing on my job...doing exactly all I could to the best of my ability to focus on what I had been assigned to do by the captain. Well, we kept going and about the middle of the second chukker it hit me...holey crap!!! I was not doing the second assignment...at all...in fact, I had gotten so wrapped up in trying to mark Memo Gracida, an absolute legend and extremely skilled player and horseman, that I completely forgot to take his brother Carlos when the play changed and we were on offense. Oh my gosh I felt so stupid...how did I mess that up! I was mortified at my mistake. Thankfully, nobody had said anything to me. In fact, the two teammates were so on fire at each other the first chukker that I had thought they hadn't even noticed me and my monstrous mistake, so I was off the hook. It was so heated, their discussion, that I had even had given them some space when changing horses and at the tent when we arrived after the first and second chukker so they could sort it out. So, now that I had realized this epic failure in the privacy of my own mind lol, I immediately dialed all of my attention to the two jobs and for the rest of the game, hit my mark in doing the best I could up against two of the world's greatest players. I loved jobs like that, because they present such a challenge in focus and to be able to keep up with players of that caliber. To me that is the fun part. Anyway, back to my mistake. I knew I did it, but it appeared no one else noticed, so I was off the hook, but boy did it make me snap to my best game when I realized what I needed to fix and how big of a mistake I was making. The whole strategy of the game relied a lot on my team captain being able to get by them in offense un touched and to be able to retrieve their intended pass like an interception on their knock-ins, so my job meant a lot to the plan we had talked about in the team meeting the night before. Talk about a new found focus. I mean I dug in and went to each of them even harder and with more precision than I had ever done before, because I wanted to get it right for the rest of the game, just like I had been asked. Great news, we won the finals and off to a private asado for the players and grooms at the barn that evening we went. I knew the jobs he had given me were tough, but that was the kind of job I thrived on for the amount of concentration it took and the fun of playing against players of their caliber. To me that was an absolute honor to be asked to do such a tough job and then to be able to play against those kind of champions. That was my dream come true. That's why I was so gutted when I had realized my mistake halfway into the second chukker and that is what drove me to really dig in even harder to fix my horrific stupid mistake…which thank God only I knew about. Well, not so fast. The asado was great until I got a nod from my team captain who was over by the barn aisle in a private chat with the second in command 9 Goaler. Still it seemed they were trying to sort something out. Why did I get the wave to come over into the middle of that, I was thinking...oh well, let's go find out. As I walked up on them, they both had quite a serious stare going on as this question came out of my team captain's mouth. "Sunny, why didn't you take Carlos in the first chukker and a half?" Oh sh#!!! It was noticed!!! Lol...now what? As you could cut the air with a knife it was so thick and so quiet you could have heard a mouse sneeze in a stall, with the second in command looking hard down at me waiting for the answer as if something big rode on my response. So I told him the truth as I had exposed it to only myself up until that moment...the whole excellent move and it went like this. "Because I forgot."

My team captain was Adolfo Cambiaso.

You think I didn't feel stupid? Talk about stupid on steroids lol!!! Oh well, what are you going to do; improving is about knowing what actually went wrong so you can fix it. That is one of the coolest things I admire about Adolfo Cambiaso is he truly wants to get to the right answer in mistakes, because the right answer produces the best results when you overcome the mistake. So there is was, the truth confessed. Then came the best story EVER. After a moment of dead silence in the dark except the firelight of the asado, the second in command laid out the troubling issue of the game that they had been arguing about. Adolfo thought second in command had changed the game plan and instructed me with a different plan than the original two job plan he had given me in the team meeting the night before…and that is why they were arguing. Oh my gosh, I started laughing and so did Adolfo. What a lesson. A top player like him thrives on the right answer to what is going wrong and fixing the weakness, because he knows that the best route to victory is to close the gaps and fix the real mistakes. They do it with every single element with their horses, with their hitting, with their team, with their strategy…all of it. That's what makes a champion like him superior; they work at learning and fixing what is not working.

Talk about going to the whip on fixing what I discovered, man was that a funny stupid mistake that got fixed in a hurry, because of the perspective I chose to have about it and had a great game as a result of my new found focus lol! I could have taken the perspective to feel stupid, angry or get frustrated at what a disaster I had just created and how embarrassing to make it into the finals on the number one Sunday field in front of a few thousand people and let it ruin my focus for a few chukkers, seeing as my team mate was counting on me and the fire burning at the tent was the first clue to just how bad of a mistake it was for the team, but instead I simply realized the mistake, made the adjustment and let the mistake fuel my effort to perfect the task to the best of my ability.

"How you let things effect you is everything. It is all up to you. Always be thinking next play, what can I do better. Excuses are wasted energy spent in the wrong direction."

This step in the process can be the absolute best one if you really want to excel. Start looking at your personal performance like a crime scene investigation. Think of yourself as the detective who is in charge of discovering ALL of the hidden details as to what happened on the field. Start to do this for losses and wins and you'll be amazed at what you will start discovering. It's important to know why you won and why you lost. Start to look at your performance without taking it personal and you are on your way to serious improvement and way beyond the average. The goal is to just figure out what went wrong and then fix it by doing the homework necessary to overcome the mistake so it doesn't happen again.

"Don't stay stuck on the emotions of the mistake except to let it fuel you to try harder in the next play to execute it correctly. That is what being a champion is all about. "

A loss means you were missing an ingredient or maybe a few. Losses can be your greatest teachers if you take the time to discover what actually happened to cause the loss. Once you find the answer then you can go to work on fixing or improving the issue. That is what constructive critiquing is all about. Try to get game videos as often as possible and start watching them for clues. If you have the ability to get a professional or a team mate who is better than you to watch it with you and help point out your mistakes, that can be the best medicine.

If you are having a hard time mastering this skill to critique yourself well or to be able to do it in a positive way then start looking for help. Look for a professional player or a coach who can start pointing out what they see. Also try asking a player you look up to that you get to practice with. My point, start looking for ways to pull yourself out of the habit of just letting it go and start digging the weaknesses up so you can address them one by one in a positive way. Make an effort to start small and then work up to the big issues. Each one that you solve will add a whole new level of confidence and that is a new habit you will start to love and live by when it starts to produce results that can be felt in your games.

Every single item you choose to ignore is one more reason why your Handicap is not moving up. One detail, one issue, one step at a time, it will happen if you get to work on it. Best type of work you will ever do ☺.

STEP SEVEN IN THE PLAN

Repeat

Yes, repetition and lots of it. Improving your Handicap is a process of repeating this 7 Step Plan I have shown you, until you start feeling the changes start to happen. It takes some time to see huge results, but it takes one day and one good session working on one particular topic to change your whole outlook on your potential. That new outlook is your gasoline and it will be found buried in the repetition, one nugget at a time.

"Trust me when I say the second you discover some visible improvement based on your own ability to create it...you will be hooked and the smile will not be able to be wiped from your face with this new found knowledge. The doors it will open to new possibilities in your game are endless."

Each small door that is opened by the process of repeating something until you feel confident will be like a bright light shining through a cracked door. To really hit your best potential you will continue to repeat this process until you start to see and feel solid improvements in each key element. As you do enough repetition and continue to seek knowledge on the subjects that challenge you, you will start to master certain ingredients and can then focus on the next ones you are still missing or the ones that still challenge you. Kind of like being a collector, once you have attained one item on the list in your personal construction zone, you can check it off and get to work on collecting the next one that attracts you. With each time you repeat the new habit of looking at things this way, you will begin to find your own pattern to self-improvement. Each person has their own way of learning things, but this 7 Step Plan and process is the formula to get things rolling for you. It is an absolutely fun process to work through and it is a proven plan that can help you get to your highest Handicap potential. I know it works, because this is the process I used and with no short cuts. I just did the work and eventually it paid off greater than I could ever have imagined.

Repeat the process until you fine tune your skills one by one and are ready to take the next step up confidently. Repetition in the correct moves and plays builds confidence. Confidence opens the door to more plays in a game situation. More plays open the door to a greater capacity to have an actual effect on the outcome of the game. That is the group of players you want to be noticed with, the ones that are making waves and affecting the outcomes of a game in a positive way. You see it doesn't matter how small the first move of confidence is that you received from the plan and process. That one move will affect your overall performance and that is how you start to have a bigger effect and larger role in the overall game dynamics. Each and every single move you are able to execute properly makes a statement about you as a player.

What's the statement you're generating now vs. the statement you would like to be as a polo player in action? There is your destination, now get to work on it.

Now listen close...

The 7 Step Plan that works, that I have just explained to you is what will lead you to your best chance of success in actually seeing an increase in your personal skills and Handicap. This plan takes one solid main ingredient to work. Just one. You, have to actually start implementing it by doing the work.

> *"Don't be afraid of hard work,*
> *within it lies your Handicap potential."*

There is no other way to improve yourself on a regular basis without actually doing the work, so don't try to fool yourself with a bunch of fun stuff that doesn't amount to much. Just go to work on what you are able to or appeals to you at the moment, depending on what stage of the game you are at and see where it takes you. I guarantee you one thing. Your game will change for the better if you implement the plan I have described and actually do the work. In fact, I know it can help improve you as a player, because that is exactly what I did in my career and the work ethic ingredient was the largest ingredient I put into it. I didn't have a manual to go by or a nice template to follow for what I was after, so I had to figure it out. I am here to help you understand just what it takes and show you a plan of action that you can start taking today to get you headed in the right direction as a polo player and to being your absolute best. What I wanted to achieve in the sport of Polo was unheard of at the time I set out to do it, in fact it was downright crazy talk and if you had asked anyone they would have said,"that is completely impossible!" Luckily I didn't share my dream with anyone and didn't bother to ask anyone either… I just went to work on it as I saw it. This is the actual method that I used and I know works, so get after it and good luck!

Remember this fact about the plan I have explained to you, the amount of work you are willing to put into the process is exactly what you are able to get out of it. I know these details I have lined out work, because they worked for me as a professional. How well did they work? When you are a professional player and the number one player in the world calls to hire you more than once…that's how you know.

~ 4 ~

More Details on the Ingredients

INGREDIENT #1

Riding

*"Learning to ride should be your absolute first priority
in improving yourself in the sport of Polo"*

Whether you are brand new to the game or a seasoned player, there is always room for improvement in the riding department. This is the place to spend extra hours if you have them and here is why. Being able to get to the destination you have in mind on the polo field is step one in a game. Step two is, what are you able to do when you get there? Knowing how to get your horse to the ball and around the field is going to be the difference between showing up as an effective player or looking like a participant in a trail ride.

To get to a play, you have to know how to ride. To hit the ball well, you have to feel safe and comfortable enough on a horse to be able to rotate your body properly. To outrun an opponent on the field you have to be brave enough and confident on the horse at speed to pull the trigger to run, knowing with confidence you can stop when it's over. To stop and turn with the ball and not lose it, takes confidence in your ability to control the horse while you play keep away with your opponent. Does this help point out some clues to issues you may be having in a game and what the cause of the real issue may be? Remember, my goal in this book is to help you find your own clues that will help improve your Polo.

Your ability to ride will be the foundation for everything else to be built on as a polo player. Without the ability to ride well, you are a false alarm in the wow department. Whether you own your own horses, are renting horses, borrowing horses or just starting to take polo lessons, riding is step number one. It is extremely important to know how to physically connect with a horse safely and effectively in a game at all speeds and that will remain a constant need throughout your polo career at all levels of the game.

Riding is everything to a solid foundation and the area to give as much extra time to as possible so you can build as much confidence as possible. Confidence will enable you to engage in as many plays as possible when it's game time and that's the way to improve as a player on the fast track. When you are a confident rider on the field you are willing to mix it up a bit more than a timid rider. This is true at all levels of the sport.

"The weaker the rider, the less confident they are to actually take on a better player. Taking on better players is what improving is all about."

Playing against a more timid rider is also like taking candy from a baby for a seasoned professional with exceptional riding skills. The seasoned rider will outdo the timid rider almost every time and eventually get them to foul or stop trying based on the fear that the timid rider has, about making another mistake in front of the superior rider. That buffer zone created between the seasoned rider and the timid rider, because of a weak riding skill, is the zone you need to be able to penetrate. You need to be in that opponent's face and matching his or her every move if you're serious about improving your Handicap. Solid riding takes time to accomplish, but that is the fun part about the work it takes to be good in Polo.

If any of these clues that I'm pointing out are applying to what is happening to you on the field currently, I suggest you start to consider this fact. If you will go spend time practicing what is difficult for you in the riding department, off the field, just think of how many new moves you will be able to make the next time you play. Those extra plays will add up to a lot over time and that is how you add extra punch to your game little by little over time. That is why there is so much value to be had for the people who are willing to put the hours in on improving their riding skills.

"Don't leave your riding to chance and just hope it will improve after your soreness goes away, go to work at it. "

Exceptional riding skills are one of the ingredients that all great players share in common. Great players have spent hundreds of hours in this department to become one with the horse, which allows them to maneuver through traffic at all speeds with complete confidence when others tremble. Great players also know what type of horse their riding is best suited for and they aim to have only those types of horses in their own string or horses they play. This level of riding skills and confidence also means they have the ability to reach for shots that the average player will not even dare to think about. In addition, their riding skills allow them to maneuver through tricky and tight situations with pinpoint accuracy, leaving average riders in the dust or grabbing for the brakes and giving up when the direction of the game changes abruptly.

Your riding is also step one to being able to concentrate on the strategy of the game. If you are not secure on the back of a horse, no matter what your skill level, it is the same issue. Instead of being focused on strategy and making the most of every play you can get into, you have controlling or staying on top of your horse on your mind in the number one slot of focus and that direction of focus is keeping you from being able to focus 100% attention on the "game details". Weak riding skills are a hidden detail that can delay a player's progress for years and go completely undetected as the actual reason why they are stuck with minimal improvement. That is why it is so important to master your riding skills to the best of your ability, so that when it is time to play a game all you have on your mind is the strategy and execution of your ideas, team plays and giving your best efforts to those three tasks...and of course scoring goals. Game time is for the game, not worrying about riding, controlling your horse or just being able to stay on. Learning to ride should be your homework before you get to the field and in the down time between games. If you are brand new to the sport no worries, your riding will improve as you go, but get ready for an action packed course. Polo is the fastest way to learn how to ride for sure, so just keep what I am saying in mind and spend all the extra time you have to adding practice in the riding department and that means with or without a mallet. Taking this approach for new players with limited previous riding skills, will be expediting your Polo prowess faster than any other plan.

It doesn't matter what level of polo you are playing, the trail ride analogy can apply. The less you know how to ride and the faster the game, the larger your loops to get back to the trail boss will be. You know those big airplane turns you make that leave you chasing the pack? Yeah, that's what I mean. To be a top player at any Handicap requires confidence. Confidence starts when you first throw your leg over the horse. You either feel it or you don't. If you don't feel it, that is your first sign you have some homework to do in the riding department. That homework will be the best investment of time and add the most value to your overall performance. If you are not confident in your horse you will be playing the game with lots of questions and doubts constantly running through your mind and LOTS of hesitation to act. This holds more people back than almost anything else for this reason. If you are spending time worrying about your horse in a game, you have to realize that is subtracting from your ability to concentrate on the actual game and making good plays. Improving your Handicap is about making the best plays possible the entire game. The more minutes you donate to staying on your horse, the less focus you have to give to a spectacular game performance. It's simple math.

The more time you can spend on the back of a horse the better off you will be as a player. Good riding skills can make up for so many other deficiencies in a player, because good riders are able to get to plays some players can't get to because of a lack of horse control. Just like the old question, if you were stuck on a desert island what item would you take if you could only choose one? Riding is like that to a polo player who can choose just one skill. Make it your riding that you excel at and that way, no matter what, you will be able to be a part of the game and effective, because you will be able to mark players that average players can never even get near much less take out and that is a huge bonus for a team at any level of the sport.

My point…get to the barn as often as possible and start logging some productive hours on the back of a horse learning to build your confidence in all areas of riding and at all speeds, so it becomes like second nature to you. This will also help you buy less beer for your teammates by solving the falling off question.

INGREDIENT #2

Horses & Your String

Horses are everything. Without horses the sport of Polo would be just another game. Horses are what elevate it to the spectacular game and sport that it is in every aspect. You cannot think that you can do more than a horse can do on the polo field. Helloooo. The horses you play have a huge effect on what you can get done on the field, on your overall attitude during the game and on the overall picture of you as a player to your team mates and potential handicappers, so pay attention to this ingredient…it matters.

"Good horses are the key to overcoming all weaknesses on the field and provide the greatest advantage over your opponents at all levels of the sport."

I give you one heads up about what you are about to read in the amount of detail that I am going to cover in this section. The topic of horses is one ingredient that will get and entire book dedicated to it, as the book series unfolds, because I feel horses are such a huge factor in Polo and to the success of a polo player. I also happen to love horses and love talking about them, so please keep in mind that what is included in this chapter is just for the benefit of showing you how the horses you have or play affect the whole picture of yourself as a player and your

Handicap potential.

I separated the topic into two categories "Horses" and "Your String" for this reason. Some players own a personal string and there are some professional players who play the horses of a team/patron and travel the world competing on various types of horses depending on what is provided in their professional arrangements between patron and player. There are also players who are renting or borrowing horses and have not yet made the step to purchase a string yet. So I want to make it clear of the effects of both types of scenarios for a player. The player who is playing horses that they do not own, whether renting, borrowing or playing a professional team's horses or a team owners horses, this category means you don't have control over what type of horses you will compete on unless you sold them to the owner who is providing them. Then there is the player who owns their own string and therefore, can control every element of what they are riding on the field. This category means you can have an effect on every aspect of the horses you perform with in a game. There can be a big difference in capabilities of a player depending on which scenario that I have just described applies to the player being Handicapped and the quality of those horses that they use to play.

Remember I said this. A potential Handicap increase comes form your performance in mostly tournament polo. So, if you have a game or two where you have weak horses it probably won't affect you too severely, but if this is a consistent pattern every time you show up to compete, it will definitely cast a negative view of your Handicap increase potential. So pay attention to what you are riding and especially in important games where your potential visibility is high.

For the players who do not own the horses they are playing. You are limited in your capabilities based on the quality of horses that are being provided and that show up to the field for you to play. It will be helpful if you know how to ride all types of horses for sure, but you will be severely limited in your ability on the field if a donkey in a horse suit shows up as your first chukker and everyone else is riding Ferrari's from the racetrack. Remember, as a professional you are being graded and judged every tournament game you show up at, no matter what horses you are playing so keep this in mind. People will usually recognize that the situation is challenging if the horse deficiency is really obvious, but you will pay for it if it affects your ability to win or have an impact on games. Winning games and being a threat on the field is what Handicappers chat about when it comes to moving a player up the scale, so just keep that in mind. If you are the amateur renting or borrowing horses, you are basically in the same boat. If your friend or the rental owner is giving you their best horses, excellent! But if you are getting what is left at the end of the list, you need to be aware of what I am pointing out as well. You can only get to so many plays on a polo field and when you limit yourself with the quality of the biggest ingredient, by playing a less than average horse, you have basically just tied a bunch of sand bags around your feet as you enter a big race. There are professional players who have a fairly high Handicap who do not own their horses, but they are playing horses of great quality provided by a team owner and can therefore play consistently strong games and have a positive effect on the outcome of a game due to the quality of horses provided. My point is this. You will be graded as a player based on how effective you can be in a game and that comes down to how many plays you can get into and that is where the quality of your horse being provided comes in. Just keep that in mind.

If you are a player and training your own horses at the same time, give some thought to this fact. When you play tournament polo it's time to readjust things and get in tournament mode. Green horses can slow you down as a player in search of a Handicap increase if you fail to recognize you have to make a clear distinction when you are training your horses and when you are playing tournament polo. These are two distinctly different tasks and mixing them takes a highly skilled horseman with a whole lot of talent to pull off well with good results. It can be done, but takes an extremely talented horseman to be able to read the game and be able to give the new horse what it needs in confidence and to know when to back off for the horse's sake. What slows this type of player down in the Handicap hunt is that they don't recognize that if you mean to be a player and reach a higher Handicap, you have to make tournament polo a priority as for "you" and your Handicap. That means get to every play possible and be as effective as you can. That is not always the best formula for a young horse, as they need time to build confidence in themselves as they move about the field and especially in the department of learning how to exert themselves physically without getting freaked out as they come to the end of their air the first few times. That's why its best to keep the two tasks separated unless you know how to do it properly. To be successful in either category, you have to know how and when to prioritize and you need to recognize that fact if you want to have the best chance at success in both areas. The conflict that ruins a lot of great young horses and slows professionals down is this issue right here. This issue I have just mentioned is also why the price of top horses is so high. People attempt to mix the two and think pursuing training a horse and being a player in the hunt for a Handicap increase can be mixed together at the same time. Give this some thought if you are a professional who brings horses along or a trainer who makes horses. You have to decide what you are and then give priority to that "title' each time you hit the field. So if your priority is to have the highest Handicap possible, it's time to get your focus on that when you go to the field for tournament games, if you want to have the best shot possible. If you are training horses along with playing, then start to separate the two depending on what chukkers you put your young horses in. Especially if you are the professional that has to make their own horses, like I did, really start to give attention to how and when you play certain horses in tournament games and start using the technique of getting off of a young horse before they run out of air to help skip the mistake of scaring them. Over pushing a young horse and running them out of air in tournament polo leads to a tough mouth and long term issues, that mean a decrease in their potential sale value. When you go to the field really start paying attention to the fact that, in your unique scenario, you have to wear two hats when you play:

1) A professional who needs to be seen, meaning be that person when you are on your best horses and go for it

2) You have to be the horse trainer, so be that person on the chukker(s) that you have to put in a new one or an un-finished one and keep in mind when the new horse has had enough and get off.

This will help your overall Handicap potential, because not only will you start to play harder and be more effective on your made horses, but you will start to have better quality young ones coming along that can go into your string in the future or be sold for a good amount of money. Both results will help fund your pursuit of a Handicap increase with more opportunities than the old style of thinking were providing.

Now, for the player who owns their own string or maybe you have just bought your first polo pony, let's discuss your situation. You are in the best of all scenarios, because you have the ability to effect what you are riding through proper string management, good choices in purchasing and being able to choose the type of horse that best suits your style of riding and Polo. Improving your Handicap is about being able to out do your opponents and other players rated at your current Handicap. The horses in your string are the potential ingredient that can take you over the top in Handicap decisions and here is why. Each horse you have can be improved if you dedicate some work to discovering what really makes it tick in the happiness and performance departments. That means, what you are feeding, what type of exercise program, what type of stall or living arrangement they have to rest in each night, what type of pre game routine, what type of post game routine what type of schooling, injury management practices, what bridles they play best in…all of it. You have a chance as the horse owner to adjust all of these factors to fine tune your horses to the best of their abilities and in addition you have the ability to practice riding them daily to build your confidence as a pair. You also have the ability to

119

make a purchase to upgrade your string when you have outgrown certain horses or have located a new one that can replace the bottom horse or two in the string in talent. This is a huge factor in a player's Handicap potential to be able to have control over. If you want to be the highest Handicap possible, start investing in your horses and your string management and you will not be sorry. Great horses in a string that can truly perform on the field make you stand out above the rest. Just ask any polo player who has been in the sport for a while about the top local players and they will immediately bring up the horse's of a particular player that stand out when they play. That is also the kind of chatter that gets you talked about at Handicap meetings and that's when your name needs to come up if you are serious about improving. Putting a string together is an absolute blast and one of the most fun jobs you will ever do, as each horse will bring something new to your game as you go. Your string makes a statement about you when you play and when you show up to the field, so if you want to be taken seriously than start treating every aspect of your string with their best care in mind as your first priority. It also means when you show up to the field make sure they are as fully prepared as possible and can have the best chance to perform their best from what you have put into them, in the work leading up to the game. Your string will be your greatest asset and partner in the hunt for your highest Handicap.

Then there is "The Horse". The best players in the world are usually connected to one or two absolute standouts in their strings. What I mean is that during a season when the combo is out on the field, the game is going to take a change and people can't wait to see them in action as they hit the field. When a player has a horse in their string like that, at all levels of the sport, that brings their confidence level to its highest. The player is then able to participate at a level of performance that can't be matched. That level of confidence means they go places and at speeds that other players pull the brakes on. This type of horse makes the entire dynamics of a game change to the benefit of the player who has "The Horse". That is the ultimate secret weapon to possess in the hunt for a Handicap increase. That type of horse is crucial in all player's strings and why when you recognize you have one of "those horses" in your string you need to do all you can to take care of them and to hang on to them if you are trying to be a professional moving up the ranks. This type of horse is like pure gold to a polo player and when the combo enters the field everyone knows it. This type of horse is also responsible for some players entire career highlight, as the confidence that a horse like this brings to a player is like watching magic on the field in what the pair is able to get done for a team and the outcome of a game. This type of horse has a definite impact on the potential increase of a player's Handicap.

INGREDIENT #3

Horsemanship

Horsemanship to me has so many definitions, so I will attempt to point out a few of the ones I feel are most important to the outcome of a polo player and especially the player who would like to reach a Handicap increase or the top of the sport.

Horsemanship is a relationship you will build with your horse(s). Your success is based on how interested you are in building the relationship and the amount of time you are willing to dedicate to it. Having knowledge about horses goes way beyond just knowing how to ride them and call out their names as they walk by. This will be your greatest and most valuable partnership. This partnership and relationship you learn to have will be absolutely visible in your overall skills as a polo player.

Horsemanship means your overall interaction and relationship with the horse and I mean all parts of it including your riding, your general horse knowledge, your string management skills, your barn management skills, your fitness knowledge, your horse psychology knowledge, your horse husbandry skills, your knowledge of different feeds and the effects, your knowledge of reading when a horse gets tired on the field, knowing how to mount yourself properly, knowing how to get the most out of your horses, knowing what type of horse best suits your style of play and the list goes on. A player who has capitalized on this category has a far superior potential for Handicap growth than any other single element. Think of Horsemanship as a puzzle that needs to be put together, if you really want to reach your highest Handicap potential. Each detail I have described above is a puzzle piece. You need to collect them all to master the puzzle.

Horsemanship is the invisible connection between horse and rider and it is built on trust. That trust takes time to create and build. Horses know right away who they trust and who they don't trust.

"Believe me when I say, horses take notes on their riders and they know who's who in the bunch."

From the moment you approach a horse, to the first leg you will throw over their back, they are always testing you and sizing you up in their subtle movements and how you respond. It is the invisible language they are attempting to speak to you in by their movements.

Horsemanship includes the habit of finding out what makes each horse perform at its best potential. That means look into what they are eating, what kind of exercise they are getting, what kind of pre game routine they are receiving, what kind of post game routine they are receiving, what kind of injury rehab or maintenance physio they are receiving or should start receiving, what bridles they are going in and how they are adjusted...all of it. Start looking at your string as the individuals they are and if there are places you can improve each one. Knowing how to manage your horses properly means you will have a solid chance to keep improving, because it takes horses to get around the field and if yours are in tip top shape, you have the complete advantage over your opponents who are less prepared. When a player has minimum to no horse skills, or zero knowledge of how to manage their string effectively, they are seriously limiting their potential for personal growth at any Handicap. Basically they are getting a failing grade in the class of Horsemanship, which will equal permanent plateau and no chance for Handicap increase, besides making an awful statement about them when they go the field.

My point in these few important examples of what I believe Horsemanship includes for a polo player? If I can say you need to over pay attention to one of the basic ingredients in our plan for success, here is another one...pay attention to your horses and horsemanship...too much attention. Think of it as a partnership or marriage. Your input to understanding and growing the relationship determines the horse's output. This is probably the biggest hidden aspect of the ingredients to address, because it encompasses so many smaller inner details that amount to a huge portion of a polo players potential impact on the field in a game. Your potential impact to a game's outcome is a big factor in the wow department when it comes to a Handicapper's point of view. Your horse is who will escort you to the highest level of plays that get the most attention or they will keep you from getting around the field depending on how much you know and are able to execute in the Horsemanship category.

Let that last part sink in a while, because it's a fact.

INGREDIENT #4

Your Hitting Skills

How important are your hitting skills to being the best polo player and ultimately Highest Handicap you can achieve? Let me give you the analogy that will explain it all. Let's say you are a superior athlete and take up tennis. You can make incredible moves on the court in fact you get to the net faster than anyone. You bought the best racquet and top of the line shoes. You're so fit and strong you can return a ball over a 100 miles an hour and there is no one who can get to the net quicker than you. Wow…you're good ☺! Well, except one issue. You don't know how to place the ball inside the lines on the return and no way can you do it under pressure. You got nothin!

In Polo, if you intend to have the highest Handicap possible it is important to become the best ball striker you can be. When I say ball striker what I mean is a player who can accurately hit balls where they mean to place them. There is a big difference between a good distance hitter and a good ball striker. Good hitting happens on the stick n ball field and gets you all excited. Ball placement skills are what's required during a game when you need to actually finish your shot in a goalmouth or to the right side of a teammate in motion and someone is chasing you in hot pursuit. Makes no difference how far you hit the ball, if you can't be accurate with where it lands. Games are won and lost based on ball placement, not how much distance was covered. Being the best or moving up in Handicap is about precision skills and hitting is one of the most obvious of the wow factors in Handicap evaluations.

Your hitting is the place you can pick up the most wow factor points, in a Handicap assessment by the general public and the committees who will rate you. People are fascinated by the hitting skills of players and often look at that first or let's just say that that is usually the first point of discussion that comes up regarding player chatter. Your skills in this department will also determine whether team mates who are better than you pass you the ball or not. Oh yeah, I did just say that. Better players will be reluctant to give you the ball if they're not sure you can finish what they pass you or you have mediocre hitting skills. You know that play where you know you are wide open and calling for a pass and nothing ever comes to you? Yeah, that play is exactly what I mean. Here is your answer why it never comes. In order to be really good, you will need to be one of the players that team mates want to pass the ball to that can maintain possession or finish a goal with their pass, or you will be left out of a lot of plays. Mediocre hitting skills also mean you are not usually going to be a solid goal finisher.

Getting a raise in Handicap is a sure bet if you are able to score goals consistently under pressure. Players who can score goals often are talked about and chatter about this topic creates positive Handicap chatter. If you can learn to be deadly accurate with all of your shots and under pressure in tournament games, you will have a major potential for Handicap increase. Being a good teammate is about being able to place the ball wherever your teammate is. That is one of the most impressive things to watch in a game and will score you major points on the Handicap attention scale.

Make your best efforts to work on all of your shots to truly master each one as best as you can. The more options you have in the hitting department, the more plays you will attempt to get in and the more often a team mate will look to you, to pass a ball to. If you are not so sure of some of your shots, those are the plays you will skip and as a result are huge areas of weakness when you play. Sooner or later all the details of you as a player will show themselves as you play tournament polo.

Great players have spent hundreds of hours practicing their hitting skills, which are the brightest visible weapon on the field that sets them above the pack. This exceptional skill set is what gives them the ability to score goals with accuracy and intent and from all angles. They know the importance of being able to drop a ball at all distances exactly where it is intended…and they know how to repeat it. A great player does not have a weak hitting side, they can work efficiently on both sides of the horse and at speed through traffic with complete confidence. This needs to be one of your aims no matter what level of Polo you are currently playing.

Get to work on this ingredient and make some serious tracks on the stick n ball field until you feel confidence in all of your shots. Remember this fact. If you feel a little nervous about taking a certain shot on a stick n ball field when you're by yourself, how can you ever expect to pull it off in a game under pressure where handicappers may be watching? That shot that makes you nervous, because you aren't sure how to pull it off yet is one more reason why you are still at the Handicap you are stuck at. Work to learn all of them and get a professional to help point out what you are missing if necessary, so you can start to be more effective in a game in the hitting department. Having solid hitting skills will also allow you to be able to make more plays and that is what you need to be doing if you want to improve your Handicap.

INGREDIENT #5

Your Knowledge of Strategy

To me, strategy is one of the absolute most fun topics and skills to master. It is also one of the absolute best skill levels to get to, because once you are at the level where the game is about strategy…how to overcome what the other guy or other team is doing, Polo becomes a game of chess at 35 miles per hour. That is the level of polo and player accomplishment that is truly dynamic and addicting. I have played for some of the greatest professionals and I have enjoyed every single minute of discussions pre game, during game and post game on strategy and I am here to tell you there are tons of small details that add up to whole lot of difference in winning or losing a game.

Strategy is also one of my favorite subjects, because it can be so much fun to execute on unsuspecting opponents or players who are unwilling to be more than one dimensional in their skills on the field. It takes a while to catch on to how many levels of strategy there are, so each time you climb up a notch in tournament level you will find out how your new team mates have a whole new view on how to get the same tasks done. For the player who wants to improve, it is so important to be open to learning and listening to all players who are higher ranked than you. Listen to what they are trying to explain and work to be able to perform what they are asking of you in a game. This is part of becoming a better player and a really huge factor in being able to grow and improve your Handicap through the collection of new knowledge. This new knowledge will help expand your growth potential mentally. This will also help pull you along in progress, as you open your mind to potential better solutions and more efficient plans of attack. And remember, I just said "potential solutions". Sometimes they come up with some epic failures too, but that is also a lesson that needs to be learned if you are aiming at the top as your destination.

Every level of polo you will play has strategy you need to learn and degrees of difficulty to the strategy execution; so always stay open to improving your knowledge and execution of strategy. Actual game strategy is the most difficult to master of the skills, because you have to have a solid foundation of the basic ingredients I have mentioned in the beginning of this chapter, before you can even think of paying attention to the chemistry and strategy of what's really going on out there in terms of play creation. Knowing strategy and how to execute it is also why some players always seem to be in the right place at the right time. They seem to know shortcuts on the trail ride around the field. That is high-level strategy knowledge and execution at work.

Another side effect of a lack of strategy knowledge to a polo player is this. Doubt due to the unknown. Doubt is what creates a lack of solid performance. It simply means that if you are unsure how to make a move or repeat a move quickly, you will pass by that play and not engage. The inability to engage in plays will hold you back from improving, because in order to be really good you have to know how to enter all plays safely and effectively and the bonus play is to be able to exit the play with possession of the ball for your team. It is ok to stay out of plays that will put you in harm's way, until you understand them better and how to engage properly, but the habit of being stuck without searching for a solution or the knowledge that can unlock why you are not able to make that particular play is a habit that needs to change in your routine. Erasing that doubt and substituting it for a new found solution is what learning strategy and the proper execution of it is all about. This will begin to create all kinds of new opportunities to be involved in more advanced plays in a game, instead of a being a participant on the trail ride.

How else does knowledge of strategy affect a Polo player? Learning to play your position properly and to the best of your ability requires a dose of strategy knowledge to know all of the best options each position has to offer in getting the job done. For example, did you realize that each position you will play on a team has a set of defensive strategy and a set of offensive strategy? Yes, each position #1, #2, #3 and #4 has two separate sets of instructions that you must execute in order to truly master that position. Why does that matter to your Handicap? Anyone who can truly master a position is well skilled and able to create and shut down plays on a field and that is the basic fuel in all Handicap increases. How a player affects a game or is unable to, are key factors in Handicap discussions and player reviews by the peanut gallery.

Top players know the traditional language of polo in strategy and are able to manipulate the traditional into effective offensive and defensive attacks that are out of the norm. They know it so well that they can read the opponents attempts to mix up the traditional and are able to come up with solutions to shut it down at the first sight of change. Their knowledge of strategy also has the added benefit that they do not need to run their horses as many yards as everyone else, to arrive at the same destination that the ball will be at, in future plays that are developing. They know the shortcut to the destination that the ball will most likely land in for the next play, before it is hit. This is one of the most hidden attributes of a great player. This single ingredient is what gives them the ability to arrive at the play early and you never know how they do it. Exceptional knowledge and execution of strategy is how. It's like a private GPS they have access to that the average player does not have. This is why the average player always looks like they are in a major unsettled hurry and has to run a whole lot of extra miles on their horse to arrive at the same place the great player is already standing in.

Remember this. Each level of Polo you will play will open your mind to new strategies, so be ready and open-minded as you get asked to do certain tasks different ways. This is part of your progress as a player and will continue throughout your polo career. Your skill level in the strategy department will be a sign of your Handicap potential to all players and potential handicappers that have been in the sport for any good amount of time. It is like the invisible message being blasted out to the sky like a Bat Signal to Gotham City to all who know what they are watching when you play. Knowing the right strategy means you will know where to be on the field and being able to execute it well, means you know how to arrive at the right time. See how many ways this one ingredient could be playing a role in your current Handicap and the lack of increase?

Ps...I love to pull tricks on players in a game who have limited strategy skills or an unwillingness to be more than a one-dimensional player, pure fun ...just sayin' ☺!

INGREDIENT #6

Your Performance in Tournament Games

"Handicaps are about a comparison and skill level that is attained through competition and without being tested and challenged, Handicap increase is a mute point."

Tournament games are an absolute must if you want to increase your Handicap. Think of playing tournament games, besides being a whole lot of fun…as a final exam. You've done all the homework, now it's time to take the test and see what kind of grade you'll get. Not playing tournament games would be like doing all of your homework in school, but never bothering to turn it in for a grade. Without tournament games, you will never know what your true Handicap is other than your own opinion.

You can play all the practices you want and spend hundreds of hours on the stick n ball field with amazing results, but until you actually test those skills under pressure your Handicap has no chance to improve. Think of it like cookies you are baking. You can prepare all the greatest cookie ingredients just exactly as the champion recipe describes and set each ingredient out on the counter ready to go. But until you put the ingredients together and bake them they are nothing but a bunch of potential. Tournament games are where you bake your cookies! You get tested on your key ingredients, the homework you have been doing, challenged by other players and evaluated. If your goal is to improve your Handicap, then you need to make sure that you play tournament polo and the more the better. It is also good to play tournament games at multiple clubs against different players who will challenge you with new tricks you are not used to.

Tournament games are also where you find out if you have any ability to work with teammates. Solo players with amazing hitting skills are severely limited in tournament polo, because they fail to realize that being a good polo player is about being a functioning part of a team. You know what I'm talking about, the player who wows everyone warming up and on the stick n ball field with their amazing hitting skills. Then hits a tournament game and it's like someone popped their balloon...completely in effective and deflated. That's why you have to play tournament games, to learn how to do what you've been practicing, but this time under pressure and with other players. That is the whole equation to solve as a polo player and tournament games are where you put in the efforts to master it.

Performance in tournament games is where the top players truly shine. After hundreds of hours on the practice field honing each individual skill and task, great players know how to step up to the plate into great performances under pressure. Performance in tournament games is key to being a top player at any Handicap.

"Tournament games are where the average get weeded out, by not being able to overcome the unknown that is presented to them as the game unfolds."

Unknown situations and solving them with confidence are what tournament games and great players are all about. If you want to be great at your Handicap or are seeking a Handicap increase, this is the mentality you need to possess. Learn to solve the unknown and under pressure in tournament games.

INGREDIENT #7

Your mind

"It's important to recognize your biggest personal asset as a polo player lives between your ears. Having the right mindset can make or break you as a player. "

I believe this has to be the most overlooked single aspect of all, in regards to a polo player's Handicap. I also feel it is the biggest single source of personal potential a player truly has. With the right mindset on the polo field, you can make major moves in so many directions. With the right mindset in heated games there are times when you can absolutely overcome greater talent just by having a level head as things unfold.

Make an effort to pay attention to this chapter, for I feel it is the ultimate difference that can separate average from your best performance. To me this ingredient separates good players from the great players. Think of it this way. Everyone has a brain, but how you choose to use it is the secret weapon that can either help you accomplish your goal or be the poison that helps defeat your mission. On the polo field, your mind is going to be challenged in every way possible and remember I said that. This is the most fun challenge of all and a subject I love to talk about, the strategy playing in everyone's mind. In fact, I love to mess with people when I am playing based on their level of concentration, confidence and potential cracks I see in it. Yes, I did just say that and it is the absolute key to winning games. You have to realize, each person playing has a different thought pattern going through their mind and many have a tremendous amount of friction working against them, if they are not completely confident in what they are doing or what is unfolding on the field and just staying focused on that.

With the wrong mindset it makes no difference how well you ride or how nice a string of ponies you have, you are absolutely limiting yourself to your minimum, because of the poor choices you will make. Anybody coming to mind as you just read that? That's what I'm talking about. Polo pushes every major human button we have and if you know how to handle it mentally, the game takes on a whole new twist in the fun and talent department. Remember, my goal in this book is to give you the facts as I know them when it comes to improving as a player and this ingredient is a huge source of your potential, but rarely talked about. In fact, this subject could be its own book, as there are so many factors that can create a solid thought pattern in a player that is helpful or eat away at them until they crumble if the wrong mindset is left unchecked. For the sake of keeping the book at a reasonable length given how much info I think needs to be touched on when it comes to a player's Handicap, we will just cover the most important things regarding a player's mind that I think need to be realized if you are truly trying to find your best potential as a polo player.

"Keeping your mind open to what is in front of you and unfolding, instead of what has just happened. That is the absolute best you can do at any given moment in a game."

Keeping a forward looking mindset keeps you ready to adjust and tackle whatever comes your way, with one single mission in mind and all of your potential energy to give to it intact.

"Just solve what is in front of you at this very moment and with the best of your ability."

That is such an important concept to remember in order to have your best performance, which over time leads to improvement in your overall game and eventually your Handicap. Each moment or chukker you take away from having that forward thinking mindset, is one more reason why your improvement will be delayed. If you never learn to solve this first and greatest mistake, that holds hundreds of players back from being their absolute best, you may never fully reach the full potential you have within you...fact.

After you realize your mind is so crucial to the equation for a great polo player, now we take it one step further. You need to own the power of your mind in every play...master it. This is one of the hardest things to master. The hardest part is not to take your mistakes personally and let them crush your try or worse, to take you out of a game entirely by getting upset. When you can exit each play on the field with only one thought, "next play, how can I do my best to accomplish what I see? " That is when you are truly using all of your mind space.

"You have to own the real estate in your mind and if you want to be the best, you have to own 100% of it."

If any thoughts of doubt or depression exist, yes depression, which comes from thoughts about the shot you just whiffed that was a hugely important pass or the HUGE and costly foul you just made, they are in confidence's parking spot and need to go.

Let's take a look at your mind as a polo player in action from another angle. Your attitude will determine your level of try and effort that you put out on the field and in practice. It also effects what you see as potential reachable targets for the game. Meaning, if you are upset at a play you will gravitate to harassing the person who created your mistake instead of staying focused on the game and your task for the team. That leads to a downslide in your overall playing potential for the day. Once your mental target for the day is on anything but executing your job for the team, meaning focus on horse issues, focused on fear, focused on anger, focused on a certain play that went like crap...all of those things mean you are not giving 100% attention to playing your position well and executing to the best of your abilities your role for the team and that is how a good mind gets wasted on the field. Small things happen that eat away at the positive force you started the game with until your gas tank of potential is empty and you are making cheapo an ineffective plays. Remember, your mind is what is driving the horse around the field through the game to plays or chasing down the opponent that pissed you off instead. Think about that for a minute.

In summary it goes like this:

Crappy mindset and attitude = Crappy effort on the field

*

Crappy effort on the field = Crappy performance potential

*

Crappy performance potential = Crappy to zero chance at Handicap increase

Solution:

"*Learn to own ALL of the real estate in your mind.***"**

For the player who gets nervous at big games and can't keep looking at all that is going on in the sidelines antics or trailer activity, without completely washing out, it will help you to remember this advice that will help you get your mind settled in and ready for the task at hand in your game so you can have your best performance. When it's time to suit up and you are mounted headed to the first throw-in. Start training yourself to turn off everything going on in the world except this thought as you cross the end line to get started.

"Keep your mind between the boards at big games."

That means just focus on what your individual task is for the day for your team, each chukker and all 7 minutes of the chukker. Everything that goes on inside the boards and nothing that is going on outside the boards…that is your new focus as you cross the end line to get started in your next game. Now get busy and enjoy your game! Having this mindset and making it a habit when you go to the field will change you drastically for the better as a player who wants to improve. It will also help you to have a clear and defined task in your mind as you start the game that you can stay focused on.

~ 5 ~

The Extra Edge

147

Now that you know the basics about Polo Handicaps, the key ingredients in a Handicap, the 7 Step Plan and process it takes to improve your Handicap, it's time to address the stuff that is the extra edge for players who are in the hunt for the top of the sport and their absolute best as a player. That means you are the person that is willing to put in the extra work, the extra attention to detail and the extra time in the saddle until you get it right. Each of these extra edge details will add a whole new level of confidence to your overall game and that is the whole fuel source behind a Handicap increase. The extra edge is a list of the next highest targets to start aiming for as you start feeling confidence in all of your basic ingredients. These are the things that will start to separate you from the average player and put you with the elite of the sport in process and skills.

If the amount of work I have already explained has got you a bit freaked out, then you may want to call it a day and plan on reading this chapter later when you start to see the benefits of all you have read so far. And warning: this chapter will put you over the edge if you are a couch potato and just wanted to see what it would take. Either way, these are the facts as I know them and a whole lot of fun to work at in becoming the best polo player you can be if that's what you are after.

All of what you are about to read is information I learned after thousands of hours training, practicing, competing, riding horses, training horses, buying and selling horses, training other people, team meetings, competing around the world, game video evaluations and in general a great time chasing after my dream and learning everything I possibly could about what it takes to compete at the top of the sport with the best players in the world.

PLAY AGAINST BETTER PLAYERS

At some point you will need to play against better players. This is a must if you really mean to improve your Handicap. Doesn't mean you have to take on the 10 Goaler first, but at some point you have to start challenging yourself by going up against players that have a higher skill level than you. This is how you find out the skills you are missing in an intimate way. Sometimes it is a little hard on the geo, but it is the best way to be forced to learn what you don't currently know in skills and strategy. When you are forced out of your comfort zone by moves a better player can make, you are then forced with a major issue to solve. How can I keep up with that player the next time is the question you will be left with, after you get over the frustration. Somewhere there is a detail you haven't mastered yet that the better player knows. Find it and then go to work on improving or fixing that detail. Over time with this mindset, you will be able to match the better player stride for stride, or at least a few strides. That is when you will start to see your game improve. Picking up the info and then putting it into motion, through lots of practice until you can pull it off is a challenge, but a hugely rewarding one as you master the new skills that used to leave you in the dust.

You might start giving it a try in your next practice to get things started so you can build some practice and confidence in your ability to execute on the new level of target. Putting yourself up against better players in practice will also challenge your nerves and ability to stay "focused on a task" instead of "the name and Handicap of your opponent". I warn you, there is a big difference in the size of adrenaline rush you will get when you start choosing more difficult players to mark. That heightened sense of adrenalin that comes in anticipation for what you have just taken a bite out of is where you need to be in order to truly improve, because that is the type of adrenaline you are dealing with in tournament polo and you need to get yourself used to managing it and being able to stay on task. Remember this chapter is about details to give you the "extra edge" and this is a huge bonus to you when done right.

Being the biggest fish in the pond, although fun, will stunt your growth potential because there is no challenge. No challenge means no need to expand your current skills. In order to grow your abilities, you have to be challenged and run into situations you don't the have answers for. Those unanswered situations are your next steps to progress up the Handicap ladder, so start looking for better players to start playing against and get ready for some action. Good luck!

PLAY AT MULTIPLE CLUBS

This is an absolute must if you really want to be good and here is why. When you play at your local club and come up against the same players all the time, it is easy to hit a plateau that you can't seem to get out of and here is why. In order to grow you have to be challenged. If you are presented with the same equation each week when you play at your club and the same pecking order as to who marks who, there is not much room to be challenged with un expected moves and new plays that develop in unknown situations for you to solve. When you travel to a new club you will be tested in traditional polo strategies as well as your own personal spin on things as the game unfolds. This kind of testing is the stomping grounds of growth and the only way to truly test your skills.

The best polo players in the world have been tested and many times over. They are not worried about an unknown player who is going to do something they don't have a solution for. That is because they have played against many different players at many different clubs and the one thing that will stand out above the rest in Polo is when you understand the traditional strategies of Polo and have been tested enough times in different situations up against different styles of players that you are completely confident in solving any new play that arises. That is how you get to the top. Until you have that kind of experience and confidence from playing at different clubs against different skill levels of players, each new player you will come up against presents a potential problem you may not have an answer for in skills and that can freak a player out and knock their confidence to an all time low when it happens.

Solution:

Load up the horses, pick a club and get going.

HORSES

"Horses…learn all you can and own good ones."

You can ride a donkey in a horse suit only so far. The quality of your string will determine how much you can contribute on the field, by how many places and plays you can get to. No matter how intelligent you are and how skilled you are with the mallet, it is your horse that is going to do the running and turning. If you are using horses to play that are difficult or unmanageable for you to play, you are severely limiting your ability to participate in the action.

Strive for quality in the horses you are playing. The quality of horses you play affects your performance…always. Regardless of whether you own the horse, you are borrowing horses to play, playing the horses provided by your patron or you are renting them, it is important to recognize the affect they will have on your ability to perform in a game. Learn to know the difference between a horse that suits you and a horse that is holding your game back. Make sure the horses you play are suited to your skill level and that you are able to control and ride them effectively.

Having a solid string underneath you is everything if you want to be the absolute best player possible. Never underestimate the value a good horse will bring to your ability on the field. It takes the partnership of you and your horse to be successful, so start seeking the horses that give you your best potential and immediate confidence when you play them. You want as many of those kind of horses as possible in your string.

Any doubts you have running through your mind when you play, due to the horse you are riding means one less chance of having a great chukker in your performance as a player and your ability to effect the game. Do that 4-6 times in a game and your boat is sunk as far as improvement potential.

YOUR OWN STRING

"Strive to own the best horses possible and treat them like the champion athletes they are in your daily care."

Horses are the absolute heart and soul of the game. Always learn as much as you can about the horses you own and what makes them happy and gives them their best ability to perform. The more confident you are in your string, the more plays you will be willing to get yourself into and that is how you push yourself to higher limits. The confidence you have in your string is the key to performing at your best. The lack of confidence you have in a single horse or your string is a huge factor to your lack of confidence on the field and inability to execute plays properly. Playing horses you are completely confident in means that each of those chukkers the game is all about you and nothing to distract you in a negative way. That is the fast lane to improving.

The master ingredient to consistent improvement is the quality of horses you have the ability to play, so if you own a string, pay attention to learning how to improve your string each season. Always seek to improve your string no matter how tight your budget is. There is always something you can do to improve the horses you have. Always be on the lookout for a minor tweak to your daily routine or overall horse management skills that can have major results. This homework is also the most fun and one of the largest subjects you will learn about. Always be on the lookout for how you can improve your horses by adjustments to the plan you already have in place with them, so that you can bring out the absolute best in each horse. Each time you accomplish giving a horse the best chance it has to give everything it has, you will be giving yourself that much more of a great chukker. The time spent in the barn is the homework that adds up overtime and shows itself in the results of you as a player on the field.

Polo horse ownership means you will always be presented with scenarios to solve within your string and each individual horse. So, if you are going to be diligent in one area of your homework and horses interest you, invest every bit of attention to how you can improve each horse individually and you will be amazed at how much it does to your overall performance capability on the field. That is an absolute fact to live by as a polo player who wants to improve at any Handicap level. This may mean to be more selective in your purchases, it may mean you need to start to evaluate your horse fitness program for weaknesses, it may mean you need to start evaluating your feeding program to see if it's really getting your horse's the right amount of power and longevity in competition, it may mean evaluating your training program pre-season to see if it's really getting your horses to their full potential or it may mean you need to start evaluating your horse's bridles they play in to see if they are going in the best option for the type of horse and player you are at this point in your skill level. If you will always make an attempt to be looking for what can improve your string, you will have the best chance at gaining the extra edge to becoming the best polo player possible.

When you are ready to add horses to your string, make sure that each horse purchase is a match or an increase to the talent you already have in the string. You know the chukkers where you come off the field and the only thing you can remember was how fun it was and how many plays you made…yeah, you are looking for those kind of horses and more of them. Make that a buying habit and work towards each purchase being a new one that suits your style of polo, your level of riding skills and brings you immediate confidence when you play it. If you want to really dial in on exceptional purchase habits, aim to match your top ranked 1-3 horses in your string in all new purchase considerations. If you are not using this thought pattern when you spend your polo budget on a new horse, then make sure to ask yourself why you are seriously considering adding another lower ranked horse to your string? Always remember this small but powerful piece of learned advice: It takes just as much money to own a good one as it does one that is truly difficult to play.

Owning that one spectacular horse that brings you confidence can make or break you as a player, so start looking for more of those types of horses and you will have an extra edge that is extremely powerful.

KNOW HOW TO GET PAST A PLATEAU

Most people get held back and stuck in a plateau by logging hours doing things that don't add solid improvement or foundation to the overall picture of an effective player on the field. That single pattern of behavior will set you in a plateau that can sometimes feel like no matter what you do, your skill level is not improving and that can be very frustrating.

One of the biggest causes of a plateau, or inability to get better, is that you have no goal in mind for yourself. Exactly what I just said. You have no clear and definable goal you are currently working at or have forgotten what you were after. This is a common issue, because polo is so much fun to play that you get caught up in all of the day to day details of your horses and all it takes to produce the show and it causes you to lose sight of what you would like to accomplish. I am talking deep fine points, so please understand that of course it's obvious that you would like to win games and be good, but without a clear definition of what you are "currently trying to improve on as a player", you have no chance to accomplish it. Look at it like this. You're taking a trip. Fill your car's gas tank to full, so you are ready to go on a road trip and have plenty of gas to go really far. Now get in the car and press the gas pedal, but make no effort to use the steering wheel or pull out a map. This is you with no daily effort at steering toward your goal as a polo

161

player or even having a destination in mind. You're going to cover a whole lot of miles, but you will never actually hit a target, because you don't have one in mind. This is where the plateau comes from at its source. If this thought rings a bell, then take a moment or some time to rediscover what it is you would really like to accomplish at this point in your polo career and journey as a player. The time you are currently spending does not produce results, because there is no destination and without a clear destination how will you know what to measure your progress by? That is where the mind gets defeated and you get stuck in a plateau.

If I can stress one major point in becoming the highest Handicap you are capable of, I would have to have to say pay attention to this topic closely. Maybe even re-read it when your polo becomes stalled out as far as solid improvement that you can notice. To be your absolute best, you will do yourself a huge favor to create a target for yourself that you are aiming for and the more defined you can be about the destination you see for yourself, the better chance you will have to hit the mark.

When you have the chance to practice it should be about just that, practice. Now the question becomes, what exactly are you there to practice? That may sound funny, but I am serious. You have no idea how many people go to the practice field with no plan in mind and exit the practice game with no solid improvement in any specific area and in fact they may even become stagnant over time if they continue on the same path and habit. Practicing is about picking a topic and getting to work on it. If you are an individual who is trying to learn all you can and do not have a hired professional pushing your plans along to be the best, then you need to pay particular close attention to what I am saying here. Each time you have the chance to practice, you can maximize your improvement by choosing a topic and making that your focus for the game. For example, maybe you want to choose marking a man. In that practice game, your primary job is to make marking your man top priority and keep a running tab on how many times you execute it properly. Exactly…start keeping a mental note of your own statistics in execution of your target for the day. Also be aware of how many times you aren't getting the job done. Yes, to improve takes brutal honesty and putting your ego aside for a minute while you find the real answers that will make a difference is what this exercise and new habit is all about. This over time will teach you to start focusing on a task during a game and that is a HUGE learned behavior in polo. That is also a very valuable asset in a teammate and especially when teams are forming. The fact that you can successfully take care of business is a valuable asset that many teams are looking for at any Handicap so get to work on this new habit.

When you have valuable assets as a player, no matter what the Handicap at this point, you become the target of more invitations to play. More invitations to play means the chance to play more polo and on better teams. Playing more polo and on better teams in tougher tournaments is how you move up the ranks. This is an area I have expertise in. Through hard work and mastering new skills and assets as a player, I was able to land a lot of invitations to play on teams, as I worked my way up the ranks in Polo starting from the bottom. So start looking at your practice games as a place to work on stuff that is challenging and most importantly, start looking at them as the catalyst to moving yourself forward in the game. Each chance you get to go out and practice, you have an opportunity to work on something in your "game". That type of focus will also help you pull yourself out of a plateau in one day, which may have been holding you back for years.

Case solved, now pick a new target or goal for yourself and get to work.

YOUR MALLETS AND EQUIPMENT

A lot of people will overlook this small but very relevant topic as not such a big deal. This topic IS a big deal and you can pick up a lot of small steps forward by paying attention to your daily experiences with your equipment as you go. Strive to have the best equipment you can, even if you can only afford to get one piece at a time. To have the right equipment when you show up at the field will be a huge boost to your self confidence as you prepare for each game and look around you, knowing you have all you need just waiting to be put into use. You can be a good player without the proper equipment for sure, but as you move up the scale in Handicap you will start to understand just how important it is to have each segment of your equipment up to par as far as the actual function it performs in your overall picture of a player.

For example, here are a few fine points to help you see what I mean when it comes to paying attention to your equipment and how many variations there are within each piece of equipment that can have an effect on you and your horses. These will all be learned as you progress, so keep your mind open to improvements that you find along the way. When you start to make adjustments in your equipment to fit your situation you will be providing major benefits to you and your horses. Being educated about your horse's bridles can have a huge impact. As you progress in knowledge you will find new bridle combos, new bits, the benefits of proper adjustment in your bridles, the knowledge of a leather vs. rawhide noseband, the weight of your bit, the size of the gag ring, the width of your curb chain, the difference a martingale adjustment can make to the performance of your horse, new preferences in the width of your reins due to your hand size, your preference in weight and thickness of the reins and what is easiest for you to use without feeling like you have a bulky handful of stiff cables getting in the way of simply steering your horse. You will also learn new info about the placement of your saddle, the use of a saddle pad and the thickness you prefer or no saddle pads at all, the type of girth you use and how tightly it is adjusted, the placement of your over-girth that causes pinching of a sensitive skin area and a horse to buck vs. proper placement. The type of horse trailer you use and the organization of your horses when they load up, are transported and able to be assembled based on your rig options at the field. The difference in being able to separate them with partitions vs. head and tailing them and how they arrive to the field in their mindset for the day. How you tied them to the trailer and their placement on the field side to witness the game in progress or tying the nervous one inside the trailer for added comfort in easing pre game nerves so you can help them have their best game performance. When it comes to your mallets, you will start to find a certain type mallet you play really well with that leads to more knowledge about the weights of your mallets, the density of the mallet head itself, the knowledge of a green head vs. a dense and cured head, the flexibility of your mallets, the notches in a cane, the size and diameter of the grip, the tacky/sticky grip vs. the old worn out shiny one that flies out of your hand, constantly slips or spins in your hand as you hit the ball, because its hard to hang on to. You will find more info about the different styles of boots, ones that don't allow you to bend your ankle they are so stiff vs. the ones that allow you to bend your ankle for better leg control on the horse and stability, dried out un-kept shiny boots vs. well oiled boots that help you stabilize yourself by sticking to your saddle instead of slipping all over the place as your legs swing across your dry saddle leather…all of it will start to make a difference as you start to know more. That is why it is important to keep evolving in the education department and stay open to improving your equipment all the time. This area of equipment and mallets is a fun category to work on and trust me, every small detail you can improve brings one more piece of confidence to your overall picture as a player and that is how you make consistent progress over time, no matter how small the detail is in the overall picture. Each detail matters and adds to your overall ability as a player. You can score a lot of progress in the small details I have mentioned and this category in general, so start looking at your mallets and equipment as an area to pick up easy progress points that will really help you improve.

LEARN TO FINISH YOUR GOALS

You been looking for the #1 ranked item in the wow department? Well here it is. Learn to finish your goals when you get possession of the ball. Yep, from start all the way down the field to slam-dunk! Make it count and know how to repeat it under pressure.

When you give time to quality stick n ball, you are giving time to improving one of your most important and visible tools as a player. When you are able to execute your shots with accuracy and finish goals, you will possess some serious fireworks in the wow department when evaluation time comes. Being a good ball striker is always beneficial in every aspect of the game, but being an excellent ball striker will open amazing opportunities within your game. That is why this homework topic is so important. When you stick n ball, actually take the time to practice making goals by setting up targets to shoot at. Make sure to hit penalty shots as well as shots at a make shift goal from all angles to simulate a game experience. Spend some of your stick n ball time each session putting this kind of pressure on yourself to execute, yes actually finish the shots and you will be amazed at how much confidence it will add to your game when you are shooting at goal. Giving yourself this kind of stick n ball logic will build a whole new section of opportunity to your game.

Learning how to take possession of the ball and actually finish a goal is the difference between being noticed and just blending into the scenery of a game. If you are truly looking for a Handicap increase, learning how to own the play and finish a goal is a key component. Players who score goals often, are the ones that get talked about. Players who are talked about create chatter at Handicap meetings. That is the kind of chatter you want out there that will push your Handicap opportunities. The more your name can come up in the goal scoring department, the more chances you have at a Handicap movement. It may sound simplistic, but it is the truth. In fact, ask yourself what's the most exciting part of a great game? Exactly…that one player who made an unbelievable play snatching a ball from an opponent and slam-dunking it in the goal. My point exactly. Those kinds of moves stick in spectator's and official handicappers minds when your name comes up and that is how you can get some serious attention…the kind you are looking for ☺.

THE IMPORTANCE OF NOT BITING

*"The real estate in your mind needs to be owned 100%
by pursuit of excellence in each play."*

One simple task at a time and for the entire game, not just one brilliant 7-minute chukker of it. That is your job as polo player looking for the extra edge to compete at the top of any Handicap and stand out above your competition.

I saved the fun one for last. Oh yeah, we are going to talk sports psychology now. This is my area of specialty and pure fun on the polo field, so I wanted to close this book on a subject that is the least talked about, but MOST important when a player is truly trying to have an extra edge over the pack. One of my favorite things in a polo game is to be able to crack an opponent and know when to go in for the kill as the crack appears. Yes, I did just confess that lol! Why you ask? Because it's fun to watch them melt down ☺. The more they freak out, the more it becomes a disease to the whole team until finally you have created a crack in the entire opposing team that they can no longer overcome. Game over.

It's a slow and steady process to create the crack in good players, but in weaker unsuspecting smarty-pants players it is quite easy to do. I say that with all of the best of intentions as a professional and always a sportsman, but sometimes you truly have to enjoy your work. This type of work is my absolute favorite. Especially when it can be done with no comments and no drama, just keep putting pressure on them until they crack. Move by move...yard by won yard...chukker by chukker until you wear them down no matter how heated the game gets.

Why, is it important to learn not to bite you asked? Who cares if you get a little hot under the collar at times, everyone does...is what most people think. Well, not me. Let's just put it this way. Every single bit of tension, aggression, over riding on a tired horse, over running because of frustration...all of that fun stuff that happens when the game or your performance heats up or actually melts down is...

"WASTED ENERGY IN THE WRONG DIRECTION."

Yes, that is a grammatical, typing and use of punctuation nightmare...but you need to get the point I am making here. **Wasted energy spent in the wrong direction is a stupid move**. Yes, stupid move for a player who is truly trying to be exceptional for so many reasons.

One: it is usually the cause of injured horses. Someone pushes their horse way farther than it is fit for or dismisses the tired signs the horse starts to show, because they are upset at a play or player that just challenged them and successfully squashed their big play.

Two: you have about an hour to an hour and a half to play your game and each minute you spend with your focus on frustration is one less minute you can spend on continuing to make solid and effective plays, because you are too focused on running someone down who just side swiped you when the ref didn't see. You do the math…that means less time to having a great game.

Three: you will literally send your physical state of adrenaline racing and into a shallow tight chested breathing pattern, which will slam dunk your personal air and tire you out quicker.

Do I need to go on? Or by these few examples of the damage you do to yourself as a player, do you see how that little move can squash your potential as a player if you repeat it often enough?

My point. Learn to conserve your energy; you only have so much to spend… so spend it wisely. You also have a time limit on your performance in a tournament game and if you waste a bunch of minutes being pissed off, you just threw your best game performance chances out the window. You do that enough times, you will get noticed. But your new identity will be, as a hot head that blows under pressure and that will not create positive Handicap chatter for you. Remember, this chapter is about the "extra edge" so this is a detail you need to know if this is you.

These are the truly intimate details of success and are aimed at those of you who would like the truth on how to be the best. I know this detail matters and can be extremely effective in your ability to have a great game and to be able to win games. I personally learned the value of this extra edge skill, by being challenged in every way possible as a player coming up the ranks and after years of playing polo and practicing with the best players in the world. I made my best efforts to absorb all I could in pursuit of my goal in the sport and this right here was a key ingredient to my success over time. Talk about the education of a lifetime, this was way better than any college plan and way more entertaining.

Let me go a little further in why "biting" when your ego is provoked, is a bad idea. Any thoughts of "pissed off" or the habit of "muttering shameless blame filled excuses," means you are spending a whole lot of wasted energy in the wrong direction. The hardest separation to make in your mind that will open the road to solid improvement is between self-judgment, which is basically our ego, versus being excited to discover hidden clues to improvement potential. Trust me on that fact…it is a fact and it will add a lot to your growth potential. Start training your mind to always be open for improvement. Open for improvement means you put your ego aside and keep looking for clues to how you can get even better. If you get beat on a play or in a game, just find out why and then get to work on fixing or overcoming that mistake so it doesn't happen again. All true champions in any sport know that fact, because this is the ultimate lesson to learn and the hardest to accomplish for most players. It is also what holds the most potential for the extra edge above other players when you can become skilled at this. To be able to play with this mentality is where your greatest chance of superior growth lies. Think of this tip, in this analogy.

Think of your mind like a pool of water with a faucet that pours out your thoughts and attitude:

When you turn the faucet on,

It will either pour out bullshit thoughts that lead you no where productive as a player except to get more upset

or

Success filled thoughts with actual tactical moves attached to them for you to execute.

What is in the water source needs to be clean water with clear thoughts of the work you want to accomplish and not the crap that has just happened. Your choice to decide on what water source is pouring out in your internal thoughts for the game. This is high-level extra edge top-secret info that doesn't exist anywhere else, so you may need to re read that concept until it starts to sink in. Trust me, it can make a HUGE difference in you as a player.

The top polo players in the world have a mind that has been tested over and over again and they know how to stay focused on the task at hand in winning polo games. They set the pace of the game by their concentration and they don't let up until the job is done. They also know how to mess with their opponents mind to disrupt any sense of security they started with until they completely wear the opponent down in mistakes and frustration that manifests itself in weak plays. Great players have the ability to enter the game with one focus in their mind...the outcome and no matter what comes their way as the game unfolds, they keep their mind set on the completed task of a game win. That means every chukker, every minute until the last horn blows. That takes a tremendous amount of concentration and especially if you are the captain of the team and must run the team's strategy execution and keep the peace among players as each one hits their threshold of heat capacity. This is one of the absolute most standout qualities and yet least talked about as an attribute to a top player, but all great players possess a quality of mind control to be able to stay focused on their "performance as a team mate" or as a field general mounted in the front lines of the battle. The greatest players also know how to capitalize on the weaknesses of their opponents mind and they exploit them as the game goes. This level of mental strategy capability is fantastic to witness as it is invisible to the uneducated eye, but looks to the educated eye like a large gold nugget in a miner's pan.

Pay attention in your next game to not wasting energy in the wrong direction. It will give you a new gas tank of energy to use for your goal of being the best player possible.

Always remember the faucet analogy and assess your water quality often.

"To be the best, the real estate in your mind needs to be owned 100%
by pursuit of excellence in each play."

THE WOW DEPARTMENT

When it comes to a potential for Handicap increase, I'll give you some hints on what makes people pay attention to you as a polo player. These are the top ranked and most visible items in what I call the "wow department". Scoring high in the wow department is how you can stand out above your competition and start getting noticed for the right reasons. Getting noticed in a positive way is what creates Handicap chatter about you and that's what you're looking for more of. Here are a few of the biggest points to always keep in mind:

- ❖ Finishing your goal attempts

- ❖ Organization when you get to the field

- ❖ Clean and organized equipment

- ❖ Horses that can out run the competition

- ❖ Horses that can out handle your opponents

- ❖ Solid and consistent performance in tournaments

- ❖ Above average ability to ride at all speeds

- ❖ Ability to play well with all types of team mates

- ❖ Sportsmanship & ability to focus under pressure

- ❖ Ability to win without game fixing, but by talent

❖ Ability to play well at multiple game levels

❖ Above average knowledge & execution of strategy

❖ Your ability to be successful in marking a man

❖ Ability to ride borrowed horses really well

❖ Horses that shine and are well conditioned

❖ Your ability to be accurate & consistent in hitting

❖ Your ability to maintain possession of the ball

❖ Your ability to know when to release the ball

❖ Finishing your goal attempts with certainty

❖ Consistently winning games

❖ Horses that stand out above the rest in a game

If you really want to have an impact at your polo association's next handicap meeting then start giving these tips some real consideration when you go to the field. Start matching your tournament and practice game appearances up against the list in the wow department and see where you measure up. How many items listed can you currently check off? That may be why you are not getting talked about much at the handicap meetings and why you may be stuck at your current Handicap. Now that you know what I know, let's get a move on it!

That's all...

Now get to work and don't forget to have some fun while you're at it. Remember...Polo is a game and a passport to the world if you know how to play really well ☺!

~ 6 ~

Some History for the Curious

Some History on the Women's Polo Handicap

The origin of it: Argentina was the actual first country to create their own Official Women's Polo Handicap. With the help and guidance of France's number one and most famous female polo player Caroline Anier, France was the second country to officially adapt a Women's Polo Handicap. The system France used was based on a draft of the handicap system I had written for the United States to address the compression issue of players, both male and female. The United States was the third country to officially adapt a new Women's Polo Handicap.

Why the need? In Argentina where the Women's Polo Handicap made it's first official appearance, it came as a direct result of an effort within their polo association to register and recognize the large number of women playing polo in the country who were mostly interested in women's polo tournaments only. With this in mind, it would also compliment the growth of new women's tournaments being added in the country that were gaining popularity.

How and why was it adapted in the United States? First, let me give you some background on the growth of women's polo and how it was affecting the United States. I have been traveling for Polo since I was a teenager and meeting new people all over the world and it hit me one day on a plane ride 9 hours into it, over the ocean headed to a far away country. "Self…why can't we network what I am witnessing (in all of these like minded female polo players and their enthusiasm for top level polo) into a worldwide league so they could meet each other and compete?" Well, that being said I went ahead and launched my idea for an international women's polo league in 2005 and today in 2016, 11 years later, there are officially recognized qualifiers across the USA and reaching in to 6 countries and growing each season. Women now have an official league to be a part of called the Women's Championship Tournament (WCT). The analogy would be like saying in Golf there is the PGA…well now in Polo there is the WCT… an Official League for Women's Polo Tournaments that recognizes the players and the clubs that host them with one common mission in mind, "New friendships, good polo…shared passion." Women now represent one of the largest growing sectors in the sport in the United States as a direct result of the participation of players from across the USA and Internationally and the exposure generated from the WCT.

Ok, now that you have that background information being explained, I can now answer the question of why and how was it adapted so you can know the full story as I know it. With the steady growth pattern of women's polo in the United States since 2005, I was contacted in 2012 by the head of the United States Polo Association at the time, who was very forward thinking and aware of the positive impact these women were having on the association's membership numbers and the growing number of tournaments being added to the association's roster as a result. He called to meet and discuss a new handicap system I had developed, for a potential solution to the extremely large compression issue among all players (male and female) in the United States of players ranked -2 to 1 goal. I had proposed to try the new system out in the WCT for a year to see how it worked and if it could be effective to solve the issues of compression in a simple way. I figured we could be the test case to work out any potential kinks and make adjustments if necessary to this potential new solution, as women represented an extreme case study for compression with all players ranked 3 or below at the time. The new system I had developed was very easy to follow and addressed some major issues all countries faced and in addition, did away with the use of letters, negative numbers and half goal designations in an attempt to simplify the system as a whole. Did I mention I like things simple and straightforward? Well I do. This was no exception and no easy task to figure out, but I figured with every great problem there is a potential solution if you work at it hard enough. So that's exactly what I did in the creation of this new idea. This new system uses a numeric scale of 0-10 Goals, with a piece of paper describing the skills involved in the decisions that a player could ask for, from the handicap committee, to learn what they were missing or needed to improve on. I like things that are simple and you can learn from. I believed this new Handicap system I had created could make great strides to help solve the compression issue and additionally would help clear up the mystery of what it takes to move up the scale and ranks.

That being said, we met in January of 2012 to discuss the handicap system I had created and the polo association's ideas of wanting to use it for a new women's handicap. The idea we discussed for this new Handicap was that it would be used in all officially sanctioned women's polo tournaments only and would not affect any other Handicap. It would operate on the same concept as how an Outdoor Handicap does not affect an Arena Handicap. I agreed for the good of Polo that if the United States Polo Association would follow my guidelines just as they had been written in this new system, then I would agree to the use of the system I had created to be implemented as the new Official Women's Handicap of the United States Polo Association. This is how it got started in the United States.

U.S polo history was changed that day for sure and opened the door for an even larger step forward for the growing movement women's polo was experiencing worldwide, to be able to take another huge step. Kudos to the head of the USPA at the time for his support in recognizing what was happening in this growth sector of the sport and addressing it with a positive solution.

Some additional details to know about the Women's Polo Handicap

Effects worldwide: As of the writing of this book there are 5 countries that have adapted an Official Women's Polo Handicap for use in women's polo tournaments only. The adaptation of a Women's Polo Handicap by countries around the world has added to the increased interest in new sponsors to these top women's polo events and the club's that are hosting them as feature events in their seasons. The adaptation of this new Handicap for women's polo is also helping to unify the ranking of players who compete in women's polo tournaments worldwide.

The facts are, that currently in our generation on the planet, women represent one of the largest growing sectors getting into the sport of polo worldwide. The number of women's polo events being added to polo club schedules around the globe has dramatically increased as well and this new Handicap has added to the legitimacy and identification of this new area of immense growth in the sport.

Still not sure how many women there are getting into the sport? I encourage you to do some of your own private eye investigating by asking around your polo club, polo school or mallet shop about how many women represent their customers...than you will start to see what is happening. This is the current situation happening all over the world. I know, because I witnessed it and continue to witness it as I travel the globe. You know how the story goes of Christopher Columbus went looking for spices and found America instead? Well, I have traveled my entire life for Polo and all types of events and what I saw while on that journey were these amazing female players who all shared the same passion for Polo, but were disconnected by continent or introduction. That's when I had the vision to find a way to connect them all so they could meet and compete worldwide. That was the original vision of the WCT.

I hope this has helped you understand the Women's Polo Handicap background a little better and help you realize just how necessary it was to address the positive growth in the number of women's tournaments being added and new players entering into our sport worldwide.

~ 7 ~

Who is Sunny Hale ?

ESPNW compares her accomplishments as, "Some say she's pulled off the equivalent of being the first woman to earn a World Series ring."

Sunny is widely recognized as the most accomplished and well-respected female Polo player in the world. What sets her apart from the pack, is her achievements at the top of what has traditionally been a male dominated sport and the fact that she was hired as a professional player to compete on teams alongside some of the greatest male players in the sport for over 20 seasons such as the legendary Carlos Gracida, Memo Gracida, Eduardo Heguy, Benjamine Araya, Pite & Sebastian Merlos, Julio Arellano, Adam Snow, Owen Rinehart and the world's number one player Adolfo Cambiaso among others. Sunny's most famous victory is the day she became the first woman in US History to win the prestigious US Open Polo Championships, American Polo's most coveted polo tournament and title. For that historic win she was hired by the Outback Steakhouse Polo Team at the request of the world's number one player Adolfo Cambiaso. She was also the first woman in US History to attain a 5 goal Handicap, the highest Handicap ever given to a woman in the history of the sport. She attained that

Handicap while competing in high goal polo as a professional player.

In 2012 in an attempt to address the compression issue in the United States with a potential solution, she wrote what has now been adapted and continues to be used around the world as the basis for and Official Women's Handicap and system.

In 2012 she was inducted into the National Cowgirl Hall of Fame for her accomplishments.

Sunny Hale in action / photo by Chris Yeo

2012 National Cowgirl Hall of Fame Inductee. "The women who shape the West change the world." The NCHF honors and celebrates women, past and present, whose lives exemplify the courage, resilience, and independence that helped shape the American West. Honorees also include: Sandra Day O'Connor, Georgia O'Keeffe, Annie Oakley and Patsy Cline among others.

Wins and special awards in Polo *(partial list)*

US Open 26 goal: Outback Steakhouse Polo Team
Adolfo Cambiaso, Sunny Hale, Lolo Castagnola, Phil Heatly
  *Tim Gannon- team patron

CV Whitney Cup 26 goal: Lechuza Caracas Polo Team
Pite Merlos, Sebastian Merlos, Victor Vargas, and Sunny Hale

Hall of Fame Cup 22 goal: Outback Steakhouse
Adolfo Cambiaso, Gonzalito Pieres, Sunny Hale, Tim Gannon

Ylvisaker Cup 22 goal & MVP: La Dolfina / Newbridge
Adolfo Cambiaso, Sunny Hale, Matias Magrini, Russ McCall

Sterling Cup 22 goal: Calumet Polo Team
Eduardo Heguy, Nachi Heguy, Henry DK, Sunny Hale

Robert Skene 20 goal: Goshen Polo Team
  * voted by players **MVP Robert Skene Award**
Owen Rinehart, Julio Arellano, Sunny Hale, Ervin Abel

Bondell Cup 20 goal: Audi Polo Team
Gonzalito Pieres, Sunny Hale, Melissa Ganzi, Juan Bollini

Texas Open 20 goal & MVP: Bob Moore Cadillac
International Cup 16 goal: Sympatico Polo Team
Palm Beach Polo & Country Club 14 goal League

<u>Wins and special awards in Polo</u> *(partial list)*

7 Time Polo Magazine Woman Player of the Year

Women's Polo:

US Women's Open 1990, 2011, 2013 & MVP

WCT Finals 2006, 2007, 2009, 2010, 2011, 2012 & MVP

First Royal Malaysian Ladies Championships 2012

USA vs. Argentina at Palermo Field #1

ICWI International Ladies Tournament Jamaica

Argentine Women's Open 1999

Thai Polo Queen's Cup 2012

Dubai International Ladies Tournament
  under the patronage of Sheikha Maitha al Maktoum

National Sporting Library Supermatch 2014 ,2015 &MVP

Argentine Women's Open 2015
La Dolfina: SH, Mia Cambiaso, Cande F Araujo, Milagros F Araujo
Coaches: Adolfo Cambiaso & Milo F Araujo

Win of special note:

Don King Days...the famous Buckle, Sheridan Wyoming!

Organizations in Polo Sunny has created

WCT (Women's Championship Tournament)

International women's polo league.

Mission: new friendships, good polo…shared passion.

www.wctwomenspolo.com

facebook.com/WCTwomenspolo

American Polo Horse Association

Created in 2006 to recognize polo ponies.

facebook.com/AmericanPoloHorse

www.americanpolohorse.com / www.mypolopony.com

Additional Books by Sunny Hale

Let's Talk Polo

How to Gain Confidence as a Rider

I want to be a Champion

To learn more go to:
www.sunnyhalepolo.com

Printed in Great Britain
by Amazon